OUTCOMES EDITION

for Papua New Guinea

Social Science

Grade 6

Teacher Resource Book

Stephen Ranck

OXFORD

253 Normanby Road, South Melbourne, Victoria 3205, Australia

Oxford University Press is a department of the University of Oxford. It furthers the University's objective of excellence in research, scholarship, and education by publishing worldwide in

Oxford New York

Auckland Cape Town Dar es Salaam Hong Kong Karachi Kuala Lumpur Madrid Melbourne Mexico City Nairobi New Delhi Shanghai Taipei Toronto

With offices in

Argentina Austria Brazil Chile Czech Republic France Greece Guatemala Hungary Italy Japan Poland Portugal Singapore South Korea Switzerland Thailand Turkey Ukraine Vietnam

First published 2006
Reprinted 2007, 2008 (twice), 2009, 2010

ISBN 978 0 19 555344 4

Typeset by J&M Typesetting
Printed in China by Golden Cup Printing Co. Ltd

Contents

Overview

Social Science for Grade 6

Social Science is introduced to students when they begin looking at their own communities. This should be an exciting learning adventure. Students will start to examine their own values and attitudes as they study their own community. Learning can be done both in and outside the classroom. Every individual within the community becomes a possible resource for student learning. Studies may move in many different directions as students discover more about their communities.

Learning can take place both in the classroom and the community. There will be many opportunities to involve students' families as well as other community members. The subject is allocated 180 minutes or three hours a week. This limits time available for some activities and will need to be supplemented with weekly homework. For some participative activities additional volunteer time may be needed.

Using the Student Books

Key features

The Social Science for Grade 6 Student Book starts with a brief introduction to social science. The student book then follows the syllabus strands and sub-strands, divided into four chapters.

Introduction: This gives students a general introduction to the field. Social science studies people and communities. There are many different types of social science. A selection of social science studies is covered in the Glossary. Depending on the class, there may be times when a teacher can mention a different type of social science. This may help students to understand how broad social science can be.

This chapter introduces some concepts in physical science as well as social science. It also overlaps with *Making a Living.*

Chapter One is a brief introduction to environmental science, geography and social science. It introduces some physical concepts about the environment. It then looks at how people interact with the physical environment. The physical environment changes people and people change the physical environment. You can explore parts of this with your students in every community in Papua New Guinea. It is important that you explain to students that Chapter 1 covers both physical and social science. Chapters 2, 3 and 4 concentrate more on pure social science.

Chapter Two covers social and economic organisation. Again there is considerable overlap and links with other subject areas. Icons will tell you when this happens. Details about using icons are in the section titled 'Using the Teacher Resource Book'.

Chapter Three explores culture and cultural expression. This is the core of many social science studies. Students may come from different cultural backgrounds and have different cultural expressions. It will require tolerance and understanding to explore these differences.

Chapter Four introduces integrating community project work. The integrated project can begin at any time in the course. However for most Grade 6 students, the end of the course will be the easiest time to complete this. The final part of Chapter Four starts to look beyond the community to the province. It provides a link to Year Seven studies in Social Science.

Using the Teacher Resource Book

The Teacher Resource Book provides a guide to teaching Social Science for Grade 6.

Key features

- Exploration of sensitive areas will require caution and a balanced approach by the teacher. Exploration has risks. When students examine their own attitudes and values it can cause anxiety. Comparing or discussing them can lead to tension.
- Discussion that respects differences will be essential. This will require care from you, the teacher. Many communities will have a number of values and attitudes, as well as differences. Students should enter the field slowly with wise guidance from the teacher. At the same time, exploring should be fun.
- Ensure that everyone contributes as they are all part of the community. This means every student will have the ability to contribute to class learning. It will be important for you, the teacher, to be sure that everyone does participate. A single class may have five, ten or more ethnic groups in it. You may be from a different community originally. It will be important to listen carefully to students and elders. Only by listening will you and the class work out how each particular community may function. It will be very important to maintain respect between the different groups. This includes differences between male and female groups.
- The curriculum follows a simplified social science process: SEE – JUDGE – ACT. These are the three steps for students to follow in their social science studies. In the first step, students SEE what the issue is. This includes collecting information and observation. Another term for this step is 'data gathering'. In the second step, students evaluate or understand the information. JUDGE can have several meanings in English. For students, an easier term is UNDERSTAND. We use the combined term JUDGE [UNDERSTAND] for this step. Students will come to see how this step works with practice. The three-step process includes the following skills:
  - ➢ SEE: forming questions, preparing a study, gathering information, making observations
  - ➢ JUDGE [UNDERSTAND]: analyse and evaluate the information, make conclusions (but understand that more information later may change your conclusions)
  - ➢ ACT: present the information or take action (and then consider the results again).

How to use it

When you receive this book you need to:

- review it to get an idea of the information it contains and how it is organised
- consider how it applies to your local community situation
- read it carefully to see how you can apply it and the Student Book to the local community situation, looking at the strands, sub-strands, processes, elaborations and learning outcomes
- map out your teaching and learning strategies
- identify specific projects that your students could undertake based on the learning outcomes (but stay open to projects suggested by students or ones that may develop over time)
- consider how to use the information to develop your own programs and units of work.

Structure

The Teacher Resource Book is structured in the following way:

- Each chapter covers one syllabus strand (Environment and Resources, Organisation, Culture, Integrating Projects). Details of the syllabus are shown in the table, 'Guide to the Syllabus and the Organisation of the Teacher Resource Book'. The table is located in the Learning Outcomes section that follows.
- There is an introduction to each chapter that names the strand and sub-strand, with a brief overview of the material that follows. Each chapter has the information arranged in sections according to learning outcomes. Each section is divided into:
  - ➢ **Main ideas** — a brief overview of the material covered in this section
  - ➢ **Example of elaborating the learning outcome** — one example of what you might do to add to the learning experience. You may modify it or use your own ideas for stretching students' learning opportunities. Note that class time is limited to three hours per week. This means that you may have to condense or combine elaborations. Remember that student safety is the first priority. Ensure that there is reliable adult supervision for elaborations.
  - ➢ **Possible assessment tasks** — these are some examples of assessment you can use for each section. You will develop many others.
  - ➢ **Teacher information**
- **Icons**—there are icons throughout the student book. These icons indicate strong links to other subject areas. For example, at the end of the first strand, measuring distance on a map is an activity. The icon will be the Mathematics icon. This shows that scale and ratios are linked to mathematics.

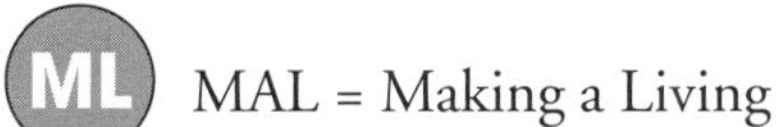

ML MAL = Making a Living

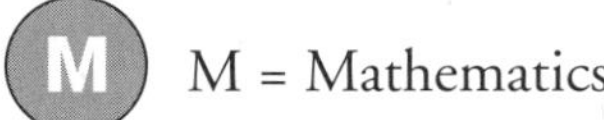

M M = Mathematics

PD PD = Personal Development

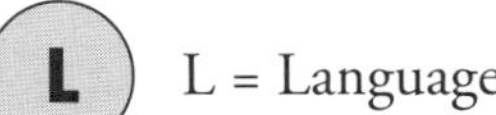

L L = Language

A A = Arts

S S = Science

SS SS = Social Science

Learning Outcomes

This resource book follows the curriculum. The Grade 6 syllabus is divided into four strands. Each strand in the syllabus has one sub-strand. Each sub-strand has a number of learning outcomes. The learning outcomes have been divided into sections. This means that you will find a separate section on each learning outcome in the Teacher Resource Book.

The learning outcomes describe what a student should be able to do after finishing that particular part of the curriculum. In Grade 6 they are designed to focus on the local community. This gives broad scope to the teacher depending on the type of local community (or communities) that students are in. The following table provides an outline of the course. The table can be used as a planning tool by teachers when developing units of work. The outcomes are broad and can be achieved in any context, depending on available resources and expertise.

Guide to the Syllabus

This table outlines the content against the syllabus. The learning focus is added to help you with learning outcomes. The title of each section is regarded as the focus for the learning outcome.

Chapter	Strand	Sub-strand	Section or Learning Focus	Learning Outcomes
Introduction	Overview to Social Science	Social Science	Overview	Students gain an initial framework for the studies ahead
1	Environment and Resources	People and Environment	The physical and human Environment	6.1.1 Students are able to identify and describe local human-made and natural environments
1	Environment and Resources	People and Environment	The effects of the local environment on people	6.1.2 Students are able to identify the effects of the local natural environment on people
1	Environment and Resources	People and Environment	People's impact on the local physical environment	6.1.3 Students are able to examine and describe people's impacts on the local physical environment and take appropriate action
1	Environment and Resources	People and Environment	Working to sustain the physical environment	6.1.4 Students are able to identify, propose and practise sustainable use of the local environment
1	Environment and Resources	People and Environment	Natural hazards and the environment	6.1.5 Students are able to identify the signs, causes and effects of local hazardous natural events and ways of responding to them
2	Organisation	Social and Economic Organisation	Social organisation	6.2.1 Students are able to identify the main features of local groups and the contributions they make to the local society and economy
2	Organisation	Social and Economic Organisation	Economic organisation	6.2.2 Students are able to appraise the relationship[s] between groups and the contributions they make to the local society and economy
2	Organisation	Social and Economic Organisation	Community development	6.2.3 Students are able to participate in local social and economic activities that contribute to the development of the local community (communities)
3	Culture	Cultural Expression	Finding culture in our communities	6.3.1 Students are able to identify and describe the basic features of local culture and cultures
3	Culture	Cultural Expression	Culture changes	6.3.2 Students are able to identify and appraise the changes taking place in local culture
3	Culture	Cultural Expression	Participating in local culture	6.3.3 Students are able to participate in local culture
4	Integrating Projects	Societies and Communities	Community student project work	6.4.1 Students are able to improve the life of the community by gathering and evaluating information about it and taking appropriate action
4	Integrating Projects	Societies and Communities	Connections between the province and its communities	6.4.2 Students are able to identify and describe how local communities contribute to the life of their province
5	Appendices	Glossary		

STRAND 1 Environment and Resources

About this strand

The Environment and Resources strand has one sub-strand, People and Environment.

Students begin to look carefully at people and the environment in this strand. Students begin to understand physical and human connections within their environment. The physical environment is introduced and students will begin to learn about the physical environment around them. There is a short introduction to geography and some environmental science.

The material then looks at people in the environment. The students begin to explore how people interact with the environment. A major task is to examine the local environment. First, students will see what natural features occur in the local environment. They will then explore human interaction with this environment.

This strand has five learning outcomes which have been divided into five sections:

- The physical and human environment
- The effects of the local environment on people
- People's impact on the local physical environment
- Working to sustain the physical environment
- Natural hazards and the environment.

An 'Example of elaborating a learning outcome' is given for each of the five sections.

6.1.1 The physical and human environment

Main ideas

This is a big section to start with as it has many ideas. The main idea is the environment and interdependence. Students can be shown that the environment is all around us. We can divide the environment into two parts, natural (or physical) and human-made.

The natural environment can be studied in six parts. These are landforms, vegetation, climate and weather, soils, animals, and geology. They are all interconnected. They impact and affect each other so a change in one will influence another. The human environment is also interconnected with the natural environment.

Dividing the environment into human and natural is just one way of studying the environment. In the end there is just one environment. People are just as much a part of the environment as trees or volcanoes. Everything in the environment affects other parts of the environment. Presently, people are a large factor in affecting the environment, but they are not the only factor.

The section closes with a look at maps. Students can use maps in their studies of people and the environment. Students will need to grasp the concepts of scale, orientation and key to be able to read maps and to make simple maps.

The following is a sample elaboration of the 6.1.1 learning outcome.

Example of elaborating a learning outcome on the physical and human environment

Strand: Environment and Resources

Sub-strand: People and environment

Focus: The physical and human environment

Learning outcome: *6.1.1 Students are able to identify and describe local human-made and natural environments.*

- Investigating interdependence will be very different in various parts of Papua New Guinea. Some places may have only a few examples of natural environments that have been unchanged by human activities. Other places will have many examples. This is all part of the exploration of the local environment in your community. The time of year will also make a difference, and this should be discussed with the class when learning about climate.
- This section starts with a discussion of physical interdependence in the environment. Using the Social Science processes of SEE – JUDGE [UNDERSTAND] – ACT, it is a challenging way to approach the curriculum. These processes also offer an opportunity at the end to revise the idea of interdependence. The concept of maps and human environments can be considered in the review of interdependence as one possible elaboration.
- The main idea is that all parts of the environment influence each other. This can be seen in the natural environment. For example, soils influence the type of vegetation that can be grown, and animals influence the soil. Humans are part of the environment. They can make many changes. Any change to one part of the environment will impact on all the other parts because of interdependence. If topographic maps of the local area are available, students may study them to look for examples of interdependence. Vegetation will change with elevation (because the climate changes). Local knowledge can tell students of the different animals and soils that might be found in these different parts of the local environment.

Social Science is to be timetabled for 180 minutes a week in all Upper Primary Schools. Generally this will allow for a one-hour lesson three times a week. In some instances, depending on scheduling flexibility, there may be scope for a one-hour lesson on one day and a two-hour lesson another day. An example follows on the next page.

Monday	Tuesday	Wednesday	Thursday	Friday
1 hour Discuss with your class the best and closest local areas to explore interdependence in the environment. Discuss what you think you might find. Consider human-made and natural features you might investigate.		1 hour Choose a nearby area and make sketch maps of the natural features. See how many landforms students can identify. Look for signs of how climate may affect the landforms. Discuss what you thought you would find and compare with what the class actually found. Differentiate what is human-made and what is natural. Discuss combinations of both.		1 hour Examine soils in nearby areas where vegetation varies. Explore the content of soils; question what is in the soil. Why are some soils good? Why does vegetation change with soil? What signs of animals are there? What protects the soil? How have human activities changed the soil? Where have the activities been good for the soil? Where have they been bad?

An alternative could be:

Monday	Tuesday	Wednesday	Thursday	Friday
As above		Combine Wednesday and Friday above for a two-hour field exercise.		

Key words

landforms, vegetation, climate and weather, soils, animals, geology, human environment, urban environment, rural environment, shifting cultivation, settlements, agriculture for cash, other rural business or enterprises, maps, orientation of a map, scale, key to a map, interdependence in the environment

Possible assessment tasks

The following tasks can be done on paper or as an oral report. They can be done for individual or group assessment:

1 First, have students define their local community. Next, locate the six parts of the natural environment within the local community. Finally, students should describe the features of each part of the natural environment.

2 The following tables connect two parts of the natural environment as pairs. Assign these pairs to students so they can be examined for examples of interdependence. Use the table to assign pairs. Remember to have students SEE (gather information from different sources); then JUDGE [UNDERSTAND] (evaluate or analyse the information); and ACT (report back to you or the class).

Pairs		Pairs		Pairs	
Vegetation	Climate	Geology	Soil	Landforms	Soil
Animals	Climate	Animals	Vegetation	Geology	Landforms
Soil	Climate	Soil	Vegetation	Soil	Animals
Landforms	Climate	Landforms	Vegetation	Landforms	Animals
Geology	Climate	Geology	Vegetation	Geology	Animals

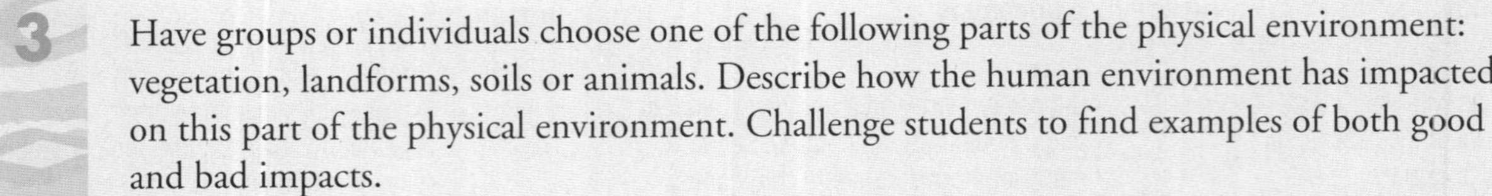

3 Have groups or individuals choose one of the following parts of the physical environment: vegetation, landforms, soils or animals. Describe how the human environment has impacted on this part of the physical environment. Challenge students to find examples of both good and bad impacts.

4 Have groups or individuals choose one of the following parts of the human environment: housing, education, transportation, or economic activity in the local area, and then describe how the physical environment has influenced this part of the human environment.

5 Explore the community language (or languages) and the different names or concepts for defining and classifying the six parts of the natural environment. Explain any differences between the traditional names/concepts and the terms we use in the text for the six parts of the natural environment.

6 Report on the type of climate that the local community has. Determine what types of weather conditions there are in the local community and report on how people adapt to these conditions.

7 Where examples of local maps are available, identify the key features on the maps: the scale, key and how the map is oriented to the north. Measure distances on the map to assess if students understand scale.

8 Set well-defined local community boundaries. Have students map features within the boundaries. Maps can be made of human settlement, agriculture and natural features. Keep maps simple to start with. A first map could be of vegetation or settlement for example. (Note that the concept of scale may be difficult for some students to understand – it will be **best if you can link this to ratio studies in mathematics.**)

Teacher information

Landforms

Landforms are major natural features of the land. It is important to understand that these features are changing all the time. Much of the natural change is too slow for us to see. Rapid change is visible when a volcano erupts or a major flood changes the course of a river. Human beings also often change landforms and other parts of the environment.

The largest landforms are continents and oceans. Students in Grade 6 will look at the landforms around them. Valleys, coasts, mountains, atolls, plains and swamps are common examples of landforms in Papua New Guinea. These landforms have been made and shaped over millions of years. Students will most easily see this in rivers and streams where the water is cutting out valleys or flood plains. Water provides a good example of two forces that shape and change landforms. These are erosion and deposition. They may be discussed with students depending on the level of the class.

Erosion means taking material away from a landform. Water and wind along with gravity can take away material like soil and rock. These can carve or create landforms like valleys, caves and basins. Erosion shapes the mountains and removes material so that mountains become lower.

Deposition means adding material to a landform. Wind and water can add material. For example, they can create sand dunes, riverbanks, estuaries and small islands. There are other ways to add material. Coral islands start from coral; material can continue to be deposited on them so they become islands. Volcanoes deposit material, particularly volcanic ash, and this creates the base for fertile soils. Volcanoes are very important to the soil in many places in Papua New Guinea.

Erosion and deposition are all part of a process that is continually reshaping landforms. The material that is carried away or eroded is then deposited or added somewhere else. People and human activities can speed up these processes. Forestry and mining can create erosion if all the trees are cut down, or large areas of earth are removed when looking for gold or copper.

Poor farming practices and poorly-built roads can also increase erosion. Remember that when material is eroded in one place, it will be deposited in another. So human actions can also increase cases of deposition. Rivers can silt up, change course and add material due to human activities. Human beings can also slow these processes by planting trees and other vegetation, or building terraces.

Depending on the local community, students may examine mountains, hills, islands, plains, valleys, river catchments and watersheds, as well as combinations of these landforms. Different landforms may be found mixed together. You may find hills rising out of parts of a plain, or plateaus, mountains and hills close together. Papua New Guinea can be divided into regions where different types of landforms are common. Remember that the New Guinea mainland is half an island (West Papua of Indonesia is the other half), so many students will be looking at some part of this island landform.

Vegetation

Human beings in many parts of Papua New Guinea have changed the original natural vegetation. It may be difficult to determine what the original vegetation may have been. This is a good chance for students to test their information gathering skills. There may be various community viewpoints on what the original vegetation was and why it has changed. In some cases, there will be no completely correct answer. For example, grassland around Port Moresby may be due to climate change (that is a drier climate has removed different types of forest), or other areas may be the result of repeated burning of vegetation.

A key idea about vegetation is to emphasise its importance. Plants produce food for people and animals. Plants help to stop erosion. They stabilise soils. Forests protect watersheds by lessening flooding and erosion. Plants produce oxygen for humans to breathe. If vegetation is carelessly destroyed, there can be serious consequences. Many traditional communities understand this. Students may be able to find *tambu* and other community practices that help conserve plants and special forests.

Plants have evolved to their local environment. This means that plant types have slowly changed to make the best use of their environment. Papua New Guinea has many different types of vegetation because it has many different types of environments. This is because we have such a diversity of landforms, elevations and climates. Every 300 metres in elevation produces a change in vegetation because it gets cooler as you go higher.

Climate and weather

Climate changes very slowly. The weather changes every day. The weather can change in less than an hour in the mountains. People need to be prepared. For example, often it is sunny and warm in the morning in Goroka, but rainy and cool in the afternoon. In the higher mountains, people have died because they have not been prepared for sudden changes in the weather. **Weather** is used to describe each day in terms of sun, cloud, rain, wind, humidity and heat.

Climate is the pattern of the weather over many years. Papua New Guinea has a tropical climate. Generally it is hot and wet all year with varying 'wet' and 'dry' seasons in different local areas. In some places, the dry season can extend to drought when water becomes scarce.

There are traditional and modern approaches to coping with drought. This is a rich area for student studies. Ideas, behaviours, attitudes and new and old approaches to drought can be examined, depending on the local community. This could form the basis for another elaboration at many points in the course.

The human environment

The human environment in any local community is everything that humans have created in that place. An easy way for students to approach the human environment is to divide it into urban and rural parts. The urban environment is made up of cities and towns. The rural environment is the countryside. The rural focus is generally on agriculture, but forestry, mining and traditional hunting and gathering are other important aspects of the rural environment.

The urban environment

The urban environment is made up of cities and towns. Cities are bigger than towns. Cities have different parts to them. These are often called zones or districts. The heart of the city is usually a central business district. This is often referred to by the abbreviation CBD. There are residential districts where people live, and commercial, industrial and administrative districts or zones where people work. Buildings, houses, roads and speciality structures like airports take up much of a city or town's space. These are good examples of the built environment created by humans. Students can look for zones in their urban communities. In small towns there is often a commercial zone with trade stores, and a government zone with government offices and services. There may be one or more residential zones.

The rural environment

The rural environment is more dispersed which means that the people or inhabitants are spread out. Papua New Guinea's population is still mostly rural. Some people still use parts of their environment for hunting and gathering. Forests and swamps have many resources for people and are used to supplement living. However, most rural activity is in agriculture. Different types of agriculture will change the environment in different ways. The good agriculturalist will work to maintain an effective human-made environment. Students may be able to map crop patterns and agricultural practices. Have students consider the three main types of agriculture and the human-made environment that result from:

- growing food for home use
- smallholder cash crops
- plantation cash crops.

Shifting cultivation

Shifting cultivation has been used in the rural environment for thousands of years. It is a small group enterprise that uses an uncomplicated technology.

Think what this sentence means. This is a farming business (enterprise) run by a small group of people. The enterprise may not involve cash but it still creates value by providing food for people, animals, trading, ceremonies, and sometimes for cash in the market. People use tools that they make themselves, or now buy.

Fallow means to leave the land alone after it has been used for growing crops. Shifting cultivation depends on long fallow periods (up to 30 years) which allow small plots of forest to grow back before cropping again. Burning is used to remove weeds and to add ash as a fertiliser for the soil. The problem with burning is that it destroys some organic material and useful bacteria. These can be replaced during the fallow period.

Shifting cultivation works well for small groups and small populations. Not enough time is given for the forest to grow back. This can result in the creation of grasslands and much poorer soils. This is a human-made environment. A simple experiment with students is to dig small pits to examine the soil in a grassland area and then in a nearby forest. There will be a noticeable difference in the depth and quality of soils. Students can see how humans can create a change in the amount of soil available. Even in urban settings students will be able to find some examples of shifting cultivation.

Settlements

Settlements are based on where people put their houses. Rural settlement supports agriculture. There are many types of village settlements. Some are clusters of houses. Another type of settlement is called ribbon settlement because the pattern looks like a ribbon. Houses string along a road, mountain ridge or coastline. A third type is scattered housing where people may live close to their crops. Some people will have two houses, one in the village and a smaller field house for tending crops. Settlements provide good opportunities to practise simple mapping skills with students. Using maps, students may describe the types of local settlement.

Agriculture for cash

There are two types of agriculture for cash in PNG. One is plantation agriculture and the other is smallholder cash cropping. They are very different systems resulting in different human-made environments.

Plantation agriculture is a type of agri-business. The object is to make a regular profit. This has a major impact on the environment. The plantation system concentrates workers in a labour camp. It may also use seasonal labour. Plantation agriculture has many more costs, such as heavy use of pesticides and herbicides that may impact on the environment.

Smallholders cannot afford the same amount of financial costs as plantations. But smallholders may also misuse pesticides and herbicides by failing to understand their impacts. The main difference for smallholders is that they can stop working if the profit is too low and wait for the market to improve. Plantations must continue to work or else they will stop operating as a business.

One or both types of agriculture can be used for direct student study in the local community.

Other rural businesses or enterprises

Mining and forestry businesses are two other operations that may occur in some local rural communities. These can make major changes to the natural environment and students will be able to detail much of the human-made environment that they create.

Maps

Maps are a type of picture. The simplest maps are sketches that can be made on the ground, on the blackboard or on paper. Maps can have many purposes. They can show types of physical features, parts of the human environment, or a mixture of human and natural features such as types of agriculture and soils. For Grade 6, the map studies are simple and focus on the local community. At this level, it will be important for students to understand three features of maps:

- Orientation
- Scale
- Key

The orientation of a map

The orientation is the direction of the map. The rule or normal practice is to orient a map to the North when it is drawn. This is to make it easier to use the map. It allows the user to place the map in the same direction as features that actually occur on the ground. It means that the user needs to know where North is on the ground and where North is on the map. If the map is accurate, another way is for the user to identify and line up features on the ground and on the map. The user can then tell where North is on the ground.

For the teacher, it will be important to be sure you know where North is, particularly if the only maps of the local area are ones made by the class.

N

A small arrow or half arrow is drawn on the map to indicate North. It is good practice to put an N or North at the bottom.

Scale

A scale is a type of ratio. Students should have some experience with ratio in math studies. There may be an opportunity for combined work on the concept of ratios with math studies.

Scale can be shown on the blackboard by making a map of a student as an example. For example, take the scale of 1:10. This is a ratio of 1 to 10. It means that for every ten units of measure on the ground, there is one on the map. If you make a map of a student, the scale might be as follows: if the student is actually 100 centimetres tall, then to map the height at 1:10, the student figure on the map will be 10 centimetres tall. Remember that the ratio is the same whatever unit of measure is used. So if it is millimetres, and a student is actually 1200 mm tall then at 1 to 10 they will be 120 mm on the map. Ratios may be difficult for students and you may need to ask the maths teacher to look at similar mathematic studies on ratios.

Common scales on maps in PNG are:

- 1:25,000 (meaning that 1 cm on the map equals 25,000 cm on the ground and 25,000 cm is the same as a quarter of a kilometre)
- 1:50,000 (meaning that 1 cm on the map equals 50,000 cm on the ground and 50,000 cm is the same as half a kilometre)
- 1:100,000 (meaning that 1 cm on the map equals 100,000 cm on the ground and 100,000 cm is the same as a kilometre)

These are metric scales. You may find some imperial scales on old maps that are more difficult to work with. Often the map will show you the scale with a line. The line will show you what the map distance is on the ground. As students begin to understand scales, they will be able to measure distances on maps.

Topographic maps use contour lines to show the shape of natural features. They may also show human-made features. The contour lines will show the elevation of the land and the shape of the land. To measure the elevation, you must know the contour interval. This will be given in the key. The interval is the amount of elevation (that is going vertically or straight up) between the lines. Often it is 40 metres. Where the lines are very close together the land is very steep. Where the contour lines are spread out, the land has a much gentler elevation. For example, on plains the contour lines will be far apart. On cliffs they can be touching because the elevation is totally vertical on parts of a cliff face.

Key to a map

The key to a map tells you what features are on it. It may identify physical features, such as types of vegetation, sink-holes or lakes. It can also give symbols for human features such as roads and urban areas. Depending on the scale, it may even show buildings and other human-made features.

6.1.2 The effects of the local environment on people

Main ideas

The main idea is that the local environment will have effects on people. This can be seen by the way people adapt to the local environment. Students can explore the different parts of the local environment and see how people have adapted. The adaptations are responses to the effects of the environment on people's lives. Some very simple examples are comparisons between wet and dry places or wet and dry seasons. In very wet places, or when waters rise in wet season, people often adapt to the environment by using boats. Note that this section looks at how the environment impacts on people. In the following section, the focus will be people's impact on the environment. Ultimately, students should grasp that both actions are happening at once.

Example of elaborating a learning outcome on effects of the local environment on you

Strand: Environment and Resources

Sub-strand: People and environment

Focus: The effects of the local environment on people

Learning outcome: *6.1.2 Students are able to identify the effects of the local natural environment on people.*

- Teachers can guide students on the issue of adapting as a possible elaboration. One question in such an elaboration is, 'How do people adapt to the local environment?' The elaboration can then move on to note that it is not just humans who adapt to the environment. There may also be community examples of other parts of the environment adapting to humans (like rats and ants, or wild pigs helping themselves to garden food).
- Another question to build an elaboration on is, 'What are the impacts (or effects) of the local environment on your community?'

A possible elaboration for one week:

Monday	Tuesday	Wednesday	Thursday	Friday
1 hour divided into two 1/2 hour sessions. First 1/2 hour: discuss where you might go in the community to study the effects of the local environment and how people adapt. Plan for the next two sessions with the class. Second 1/2 hour: step outside the classroom and have students investigate how the school building, grounds and facilities are adapted for the local environment. Ask students for suggestions on how to better adapt the school to the local environment.		1 hour Look for examples of people adapting to the local environment. Focus on structures. For example, consider a local market. Investigate features that help people adapt, for example, shade to help keep produce and people cool, elevated areas to help keep people and products dry. Also investigate where adaptation is poor. There may be poor drainage or little shade. Have students map out areas of useful adaptation and areas where adaptation may be poor.		1 hour Look for examples of people adapting to the local environment. Focus on agricultural growing activities. In towns and cities you may be able to find migrant activities that are using systems in the local environment that came from the migrant's home of origin. You can compare these to local traditional adaptations. In rural areas, you can investigate local traditional adaptations and introduced adaptations. Have students interview agricultural people. Ask about the local means of adapting to different soils and other local environmental features.

An alternative could be:

Monday	Tuesday	Wednesday	Thursday	Friday
As above		Combine Wednesday and Friday above for a two-hour field exercise.		

Key words

This section is limited to three key words or concepts.
adapt, adaptation, failure to adapt

Possible assessment tasks

The following tasks can be done on paper or as an oral report. They can be done for individual or group assessment:

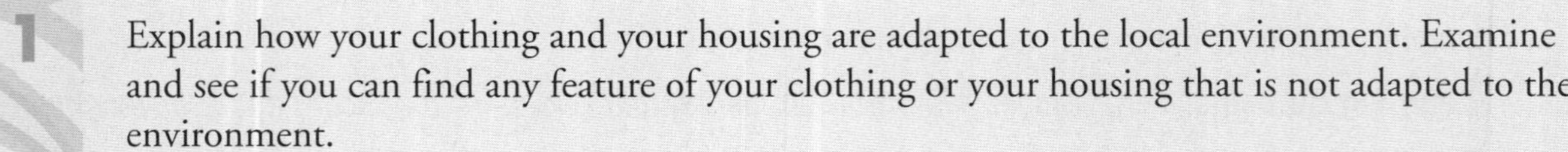

1. Explain how your clothing and your housing are adapted to the local environment. Examine and see if you can find any feature of your clothing or your housing that is not adapted to the environment.
2. Find something in your local environment that has failed to adapt to the local environment. Explain why it has failed.
3. Compare what you think are good adaptations to the local environment with adaptations that do not work as well. What can you see in your local environment that could be better adapted?
4. Compare the adaptations of wild animals and plants that people use for food with introduced plants and animals in your local community.

Teacher information

Adapt and adaptation

To adapt to something means to fit in with it. To adapt is an action. An adaptation is a change that allows something to be better used. Humans, plants and animals can all be seen to adapt to their environment. Humans are very adaptable. In cold climates they adapt by using clothing to stay warmer. In hot climates they adapt by building large roofs for shade and to be cooler, or by elevating floors to catch the breeze and create better airflows.

An adaptation is the item or system that has been changed. You will explore many types of adaptations with your students. The first use of this concept is with the natural environment. A high roof is an adaptation. A house on stilts is an adaptation to a hot climate; it can also be an adaptation to flooding. A sealed road is an adaptation that allows usage in all types of weather. This is why it is called an all-weather road.

Clothing is an interesting adaptation. It can protect sensitive skin from sunburn in hot climates. It is essential in very cold climates. In other cases, it is more a cultural adaptation than an environmental one.

Failure to adapt

Students may be able to find examples of failures to adapt. This is the same as adaptations that fail. Looking at failures may make the concept of adaptation easier for students to understand. Roads that become muddy and unusable in the wet season have failed. They cannot adapt to the conditions. Many local communities will have cases where people have tried to introduce crops or animals that were not suited for the local environment. They failed to adapt and died, or were eaten when it was clear they would not survive. European pigs are a good example in many places. They could not adapt to the local conditions. They had to be bred with local pigs, and even then, many cross-breeds did not survive.

Some communities will have examples of poor building techniques that are not adapted to local conditions. The buildings may be difficult to repair, expensive to operate and/or uncomfortable. Some sewerage and drainage systems are bad adaptations to local conditions and may cause disease and water pollution. They are all examples of failures to adapt to the local environment.

You may also find examples of shoes and clothing that are not adapted to the local environment. They are quickly attacked by mildew or are uncomfortable to wear.

6.1.3 People's impact on the local physical environment

Main ideas

People are constantly changing their environment. This has happened for thousands of years. Sometimes the changes have been short term, like small villages that settle in an area and then shift to another area. Within 30 to 100 years the environment returns to the original forest. This may happen even more quickly in some coastal and swamp areas. At other times the changes people make to the environment are long term. The forest is changed permanently to grassland, or a smooth hillside becomes terraces.

More complex technologies in both urban and rural areas are making major changes to the environment. Gold and copper mining is changing rivers. Forests are being cleared and in some places there is fauna and flora (animals and vegetation) that may never be seen again. These are major impacts on the environment. The use of boats is another example. They are an adaptation for wet environments. At the same time, big boats can now clear all the fish or lobster from an area. The environment may be damaged permanently. Similarly, many small boats all using derris for fishing can also change the environment.

In the previous section, students investigated how the environment impacts on people. The hot sun causes people to seek or make shade to stay a little cooler. This is an adaptation. It does not stop the climate being hot. In this section, students look at how people do change the environment at a local or community level.

Example of elaborating a learning outcome on people impacting the environment

Strand: Environment and Resources

Sub-strand: People and environment

Focus: People's impact on the local physical environment

Learning outcome: *6.1.3 Students are able to examine and describe people's impacts on the local physical environment and take appropriate action.*

- An elaboration can start to cover several sections now. For example, you can start with the theme, 'What does changing the environment mean?' Then look at the impacts of the environment on people in the previous section, and people's impact on the environment in this section, with students answering questions like:
  - ➢ What are human effects on the local environment?
  - ➢ How do people change the local environment?

A possible elaboration for one week:

Monday	Tuesday	Wednesday	Thursday	Friday
1 hour The students take a journey of the imagination. They try to imagine what the school grounds and local community area would have looked like before any human beings came there. They might make drawings on paper or the blackboard of what different places were like and explore reasons for their visions. What environment and what interdependencies existed then? They might make a model using bush materials — this could take up part of the second hour.		1 hour Select several places that students have described in the earlier session. Visit them and investigate the differences that people have made to the environment. Have them explore what plants and animals are different. Students can investigate what differences people have made to waterways and other bodies of water (include beaches if near the sea). You may discuss water quality and how it has changed because of human activities (this will include animals that have been introduced to the environment by humans, such as pigs). You may also examine what natural changes have and are taking place right now with or without humans.		1 hour Divide the class into two teams. Again select a few of the local areas untouched by humans that were nominated by students earlier. Have one team look at positive or good changes that people have made to the environment. Have the other team look for negative or bad changes that people have made to the environment. Have each group report their results and discuss the findings. (You may need to carry this into another week, first hour. It can also lead to an elaboration for learning outcome 6.1.4.)

Alternative schedule: adapt to your particular timetable.

Key words

changing the environment, impacts, urban environment, rural environment, census, population growth, population density

Possible assessment tasks

The following tasks can be done on paper or as an oral report. They can be done for individual or group assessment:

1 Make a study of how the local environment has changed over time. Collect information from relatives and friends about the changes they have seen. Make a conclusion about what the greatest impacts have been and explain why.

2 Choose one part of the human-made environment (village, buildings, roads, type of agriculture) and explain how it has changed the local environment.

3 Have individuals or teams debate topics. Assess students on their ability to SEE (collect information) and JUDGE [UNDERSTAND] whichever side of the debate they are given. The key to assessment is how well they can judge the changes that people have made to the environment. (Note: there are no right answers. Give students a day or two to prepare their cases.) Appraise students on their thinking and understanding, and for defending their side of the debate. Debrief the class after the debates. Be sure they understand that there is no single right answer and that debates help improve knowledge whichever side you are on.

Here are a few examples of topics for debate.

- Stations, towns and cities in urban areas make more changes to the environment than agriculture, mining and forestry in rural areas **versus** agriculture, mining and forestry in rural areas make more changes to the environment than stations, towns and cities in urban areas.
- Bigger populations make more changes to the environment **versus** growing populations do not make significant change to the environment. The real change comes from the way people use the environment.
- Cars, PMVs and trucks make more changes to the environment than houses and buildings **versus** houses and buildings make more changes to the environment than cars, PMVs and trucks.
- The traditional ways of protecting our local environment are still working **versus** the traditional ways of protecting our local environment are not working anymore.

Teacher information

Changing the environment

Students will find that all human activity makes some change to the environment. Some is more visible or easier to see than others. It is also much easier to see change to the local environment in terms of vegetation, animals, soils and landforms. It will be harder to see changes to geology unless there is a major mining operation in the local area. It will be even harder to see any change to climate although one school of environmental science believes that changing from hunter-gatherer activities to agriculture started climate changes around 8,000 years ago.

Impacts

Impact is another word for change. It is a very common term. It is often used as part of the term 'environmental impact'. This means environmental change, usually caused by human beings. **Environmental impact studies** or **environmental impact assessments** look at changes to the environment caused by particular human activities. They can be done for mining, or planned mines, logging, dams, oil palm plantations and any other major activity that will change the environment.

Impacts increase with the amount of activity. The amount or scale of any activity will have a different impact on the environment. Have students imagine that there are only 500 slash and burn plots being cleared each year in a province, or that there are only 15 small factories in a city. These small amounts of human activity will only make a small change to the environment. Now imagine 5,000 plots being cleared or 150 factories at work. The amount of impact will grow. Each small group of people think they are not making much change, but the combination of groups of people will cause much greater change.

Urban environment

Cities and towns are urban environments. They can make major changes to the natural environment. Landforms may be changed. A dam may create a lake in what was dry land and provide the city with water. A hill can be levelled to provide construction material or fill. Hillsides can be cut away to make space for roads. A good example is Spring Garden Road in Port Moresby. The road was planned over a hundred years ago, but only recently completed after years of quarrying and removal of hillside material.

Rural environment

Agriculture, mining and forestry are human activities that make the most visible changes to the rural environment. Students can find many local examples. Removing forest along riverbanks for agriculture or logging damages water quality. This in turn affects anything that lives in the water. Mines can poison rivers if tailings and by-products are dumped into the rivers. Similarly, agricultural pesticides and herbicides can poison rivers and other animal life in rural areas.

Census

A census counts people in a population. The Papua New Guinea National Census counts all the people in Papua New Guinea. A complete census counts every person. The national census collects information about people. It includes family size, sex, age, occupation and other variables. Sometimes a census is done using a sample. It may be possible to locate census information about your local community. This should help students better understand some factors about people in the local community.

Population growth

Population growth can be slow or fast. Population growth can be positive or negative. If it is positive, that means that the population is growing larger. If it is negative, that means that the population is growing smaller. In Papua New Guinea, the population is growing fast and getting larger every year. However, this may vary for local communities. Some may have slow or even negative growth. Following the SEE – JUDGE [UNDERSTAND] – ACT ideas of the curriculum, students can explore the history of populations in the local community and discuss findings.

Population density

The population density is the number of people in a given area. Usually it is measured as persons per square kilometre. Generally, the higher the density, the greater the impact of people on that environment. To calculate the population density of an area, take the population and divide it by the area. For example, an area is 100 square kilometres and the population is 10,000 people:

$$\frac{10{,}000 \text{ people}}{100 \text{ km}} = \text{a population density of 100 persons per square kilometre}$$

Generally students should see that the denser the population is, the greater the impact on the environment. There are always exceptions, so challenge students to think of them. For example, a truckload of herbicide or an atomic bomb could make a large impact even with a very low density population.

6.1.4 Working to sustain the physical environment

Main ideas

This learning outcome starts a foundation for students to identify, propose and practise sustainable use of the local environment. The main idea is for students to actually do something to help sustain the environment. They should now be more aware of the environment through the earlier work on interdependency. Now they can see themselves as a real part of the environment. Every action they take has some impact on their environment. The key to this section is for them to identify what they can do practically to help sustain the environment.

Example of elaborating a learning outcome on sustainable environmental use

Strand: Environment and Resources

Sub-strand: People and environment

Focus: Working to sustain the physical environment

Learning outcome: *6.1.4 Students are able to identify, propose and practise sustainable use of the local environment.*

- Sustainable use of the environment is a complex subject. It is important not to try to do too much. Students will need to understand that this is a difficult area with no completely right answers.
- Sustainable use of the environment is something that all societies wrestle with. It is always easier to use up resources than to sustain them. Students should be able to find examples of sustainable use of the environment, as well as examples of the opposite.

A possible elaoration for one week:

Monday	Tuesday	Wednesday	Thursday	Friday
1 hour Following on from the class discussion for the elaboration of Learning outcome 6.1.3, further examine the bad or negative effects of human impact in the environment that the class has found. Ask the class why people might have done this. Consider ways that the negative or bad effects could be changed. Have the class choose one way for practical application.		1 hour Work on a detailed plan with the class on how they can work to sustain the environment. There probably will not be enough time to start action. It depends on the student's plan. Have them decide on what amount of time they can dedicate to making the plan work. Be certain that no one will be harmed. If any official or community permission is needed, be certain the class receives it before commencing action.		1 hour Start action on improving and sustaining the environment. (At a later period, investigate with the class what impact their actions have had on the environment. Investigate how sustainable the plan was.)

Alternative schedule: adapt to your particular timetable.

Key words

sustainable, natural resources, balanced use of the environment

Possible assessment tasks

The following tasks can be done on paper or as an oral report. They can be done for individual or group assessment:

1 In groups or as individuals, look at one part of the local environment, for example:
- Waterways
- Garden areas
- Housing
- School grounds
- Markets

Identify ways to maintain and sustain these environments and put them into action.

2 Choose a natural resource found in your local community and prepare a diagram to show balanced use of this resource.

3 Examine your home and what is in it. Make lists of everything that is from renewable resources and everything that is from a non-renewable resource. Compare the lists in class and consider how much of the non-renewable resource materials could be recycled.

Teacher information

Natural resources

A resource is something of value. Money, machines, gold, students, teachers and fish are all examples of resources. **Natural resources** are parts of the physical environment that people give value to. At different times and in different places these values change. Everyone recognises land as a natural resource. The value people give to what is on and what is in the land changes. There are many examples of changing natural resources in the local communities of Papua New Guinea. For example water, which is a very important natural resource, used to be free and clean in all local communities. Now many places must pay for water, and other local communities have problems with water quality.

Gold, copper, timber, fish, crayfish, gas and oil are all important natural resources in Papua New Guinea. There are major industries like mining, forestry and fisheries that take these natural resources.

Sustainable

Sustainable comes from the verb, **to sustain**. To sustain something is to keep it going. For example, food, water, shelter and caring sustain human life. Food, water and shelter all come from the natural environment. We can see that we need the natural environment to sustain human life. We need to use the environment in a sustainable way. This means we will be able to keep using it and it will continue to sustain us.

If we use the environment in a sustainable way we will use the environment, but not take everything away from it. Students can easily see this by extreme examples. If people take all the fish out of the river, there will be no more fish to eat or sell. If too much herbicide or pesticide or mining waste goes into a river, a natural resource is destroyed. It is not being used sustainably.

The question for students to explore is how to use the environment sustainably and what can they do practically to assist this. Much will depend on the local community. In almost every case, however, students can help to improve the environment. Improvements will help the sustainable use of the environment. For example, stopping litter from entering waterways or the sea improves the environment. Helping trees and plants to grow by preventing unnecessary burning can help the environment. There are many other simple actions that can help sustain the environment.

Students may think that, by themselves, they can have very little impact on the environment. It is important to understand the idea of scale and sustainable use. If just one person puts a litre of poison or pollution into the sea or a river, it is very little each day. But if each person does this, then 30 persons will put 30 litres a day into a small village stream. This could happen 365 days a year. A thousand people or ten thousand people increase the magnitude of the scale. But it all starts with one person. So each student will have an impact.

The same example can be seen in setting fires. If just one person sets grass fires for no reason, it does some damage. If everyone starts setting fires for no reason, the scale of damage can grow to be very large. The grass fires spread to forest and damage trees, so soil is unprotected and erodes away. Animals will suffer and soil may be lost forever with many plants never returning to that environment.

Balanced use of the environment

Sustainable use of the environment requires balance. This means both taking and giving. Some trees can be taken but others should be given time to grow to replenish the ones that are taken. Another option is to protect entire areas.

Unbalanced use of the environment is dangerous. It makes people more susceptible because they rely on a limited environment. For example, it would be unbalanced use if the entire coast of Papua New Guinea was planted in coconuts. When the copra price was high, there would be plenty of money. However, as soon as the price dropped, people would be in trouble. Worse, a coconut disease could threaten the entire coconut environment.

This type of extreme example shows the need for balance. The challenge for students will be to find a good balance. Remind students that people and the environment are always changing, so there can be more than one good answer.

Renewable resources

To renew is to make something new again. Much traditional use of the environment was renewable. The scale was small, so the impact was small. For fishing, people could use derris root and not do much damage. Today, there are too many people and fish are poisoned faster than the fish can be renewed. The key to renewable resources is taking good care of them. This means balanced use. Other examples of renewable resources are the forest, mangroves, water and agriculture. Some types of power are renewable, for example solar power from sunlight, wind, hydropower and tides. However, a balanced approach must still be taken with power and other renewable resources, or they will also result in big problems. Poorly designed and maintained hydropower dams may silt up for example.

Non-renewable resources

Other resources cannot be renewed. Non-renewable resources include mining products like copper, gold and oil. They can't be replaced once they have been removed from the ground. They are not renewable. In some cases these resources can be recycled or reused, but these resources have normally already been removed from Papua New Guinea. This means that the money made from their sale needs to be used wisely to sustain other activities.

Finally, all resources can be used in non-sustainable ways. Fish can be taken from lakes, rivers and seas faster than they can breed to replace themselves. Forests can be cleared and environments destroyed with animals and plants lost forever. Water can be poisoned with chemicals which could take hundreds of years to remove. These are all examples of using resources in a non-renewable way.

6.1.5 Natural hazards and the environment

Main ideas

Natural hazards are a part of life. Some people call them natural disasters. They are a disaster when people are not prepared. If people have carelessly changed the environment, the disasters can be even worse. Normal flooding can become catastrophic when too much logging has altered the watershed. Another example is when people build in areas that are subject to natural hazards. Building homes on unstable mountain slopes or placing towns too close to volcanoes means natural hazards can become possible disasters.

Learning to live with natural hazards is important. They are part of the environment. People can adapt in many ways. Towns and villages can be carefully located. Houses can be built in a special way so they are protected against flooding, volcanoes, earthquakes, tsunamis and other hazards. Villages can have warning systems and the inhabitants can pay attention to past events and traditional knowledge.

Students can protect themselves by understanding local natural hazards and how to deal with them. It will be important for students to seek traditional local knowledge and scientific knowledge.

Example of elaborating a learning outcome on natural hazards

Strand: Environment and Resources

Sub-strand: People and environment

Focus: Natural hazards and the environment

Learning outcome: *6.1.5 Students are able to identify the signs, causes and effects of local hazardous natural events and ways of responding to them.*

A possible elaboration for one week:

Monday	Tuesday	Wednesday	Thursday	Friday
1 hour Divide the class into work groups. Have each group choose a local natural hazard. Each group then discusses how to build a model of the natural hazard they have chosen. They agree on what bush materials each one can bring to make the model.		1 hour Students make a model of the natural hazard chosen by their work groups. At home they collect stories about this particular natural hazard and how the community copes with it.		1 hour Each group presents its model and reports on the signs, causes and effects of the hazard. They present a summary of their families' stories on how to deal with the hazard, and the effect of this natural hazard on people.

Alternative schedule: adapt to your particular timetable.

Key words

natural hazards, cyclones, drought, earthquakes, fire, floods, frost, landslides, tsunamis, volcanic eruptions

Possible assessment tasks

The following tasks can be done on paper or as an oral report. They can be done for individual or group assessment:

1. Research two natural hazards in your local community. Find local stories and local traditional knowledge about these two hazards and how to respond to them. Interview three different people who have been through the hazard and examine their stories. What would they do differently now? Write or explain how you would respond to the two natural hazards and tell why in each case.

2. Group assessment: Divide the class into two or more groups. Tell one group the name of a natural hazard, without letting the other group or groups know. Have the group act out how to properly respond to the hazard. Have the other group or groups identify the hazard and comment on the response. (Was the response good or bad? What else could be done?) Give all groups a turn at acting out a response to a natural hazard.

Teacher information

Natural hazards

Natural hazards are a part of life in Papua New Guinea. There are different hazards that threaten different local communities. Examples of hazards include cyclones, drought, earthquakes, fire, floods, frost, landslides, tsunamis and volcanic eruptions. Natural hazards may have both good and bad effects. People often focus on the bad effects since they can cause loss of life, but there are good effects as well. For example, volcanoes may create very productive soils; floods can replenish waterholes and improve soils by leaving silt; storms can bring water and flooding; and storm damage can give opportunities for new growth vegetation.

Cyclones

Cyclones are major storms in tropical seas that draw energy from warm seawaters. They weaken over land.

Drought

Droughts are long periods of dry weather. Drought is marked by unusually low rainfall for the area. Drought is different from a dry season, because the dry season is part of the expected climate pattern. Drought is not expected on a regular basis, but past events can indicate a pattern of how likely it may be.

Earthquakes

Earthquakes result from movements deep within the earth. Some places are much more prone to earthquakes because of the regional geology. Technically, this is part of the theory of plate tectonics, which studies the huge plates beneath the earth's surface. Where these plates meet, earthquakes are common.

Fire

As a natural hazard, fires are caused by lightning strikes, and natural gas leaks in some cases. Many fires are actually a human-made hazard.

Floods

Floods are higher than expected levels of water. Some places flood regularly. Floods can be caused by high rainfall, quick runoff of rainfall from the land, storm surges of coastal waters, and combinations of high rainfall and high tides along the coast. Many Papua New Guineans regularly face this natural hazard.

Frost

Frost is created when temperatures drop below freezing and dew freezes. Frost can kill or damage crops that are not used to frosty conditions.

Landslides

Landslides or landslips generally occur when water loosens the ground on steep slopes and acts as a lubricant for the land to slide.

Tsunamis

Tsunamis are huge waves caused by earthquakes beneath the sea. They are of no danger until they hit shallow shores.

Volcanic eruptions

Cracks that go deep into the earth's surface allow molten rock (rock that has melted because of heat) to push up toward the surface. This can result in various types of eruptions and other hazards to human life.

STRAND 2

Organisation

About this strand

The Organisation strand has one sub-strand, Social and Economic Organisation. These are large subject areas. Students will begin to learn basic ideas about the organisation of society and the economy. They will explore these themes in their local communities. Material is separated for simplicity. In real life social and economic organisation are mixed together and students may be able to make some of these connections as the study progresses.

This strand has three learning outcomes which have been divided into three sections:

- Social organisation
- Economic organisation
- Community development

The sections are used to present the material more easily. The learning outcomes overlap. They are complex and have been simplified for students. By the end of the strand, students may better understand some of the overlap.

An 'Example of elaborating a learning outcome' is given for each of the three sections.

Organisation

6.2.1 Social organisation

Main ideas

Everyone is born into a society. Some people may spend their whole lives with little thought about how the society is organised. Others learn about society and try to benefit from this knowledge. Papua New Guineans can see a number of different societies blending around them. Students will be able to identify different traditional groups and different introduced groups. This section introduces some basic concepts about studying and understanding groups in the local society. It introduces the basics of social organisation or how communities are organised to students.

There are many ways to study social organisation. It is important to understand that everyone has some values that differ, which will affect the way they look at their own and other groups. When working with students the most important idea is to build respect for groups and ways of thinking that are different. Two major areas are religious and ethnic differences. Students will find these in their own communities. By looking at these in terms of roles, rights, responsibilities, attitudes and values, students will be given tools to better understand social organisation.

Example of elaborating a learning outcome on local groups

Strand: Organisation

Sub-strand: Social and economic organisation

Focus: Social organisation

Learning outcome: *6.2.1 Students are able to identify the main features of local groups and the contributions they make to the local society and economy.*

- Elaborations can be based on inviting guests to the school. Different themes can be followed depending on which guests are willing to come to speak to students and be questioned by them. Have students work on questions based on text ideas before guests come. Be certain to brief guests on the learning outcome topics and text material so they can prepare their short talks accordingly.
- Another elaboration is for students to interview community members outside the school.

A possible elaboration for one week:

Monday	Tuesday	Wednesday	Thursday	Friday
1 hour Start with a class discussion about important groups in the local community. Discuss issues, for example: What are the most important groups? Who is in them? What values do you think they have? How do they help the community? Do some groups not help the community? Have students list the most important groups.		1 hour Prepare a plan with the class for interviewing a selection of community groups that they think are important. Have the class agree on five questions that they would like to ask members in the important groups. Divide the class into interviewing groups. Have the class interview members in several important groups. Have them prepare summaries of the interviews. [Note be sure to limit the number of questions. It is always easy to collect too much and not have enough time for comparisons or summaries.]		1 hour Have each set of class interviewers report back to the class about the group members they interviewed. What values did they find? How do the groups help the community? Have a class discussion comparing the findings of the different interview sets. [It will generally be best for boys to interview males and girls to interview females. Ensure student safety; keep student interview groups with a responsible adult. This elaboration may take more time than one week.]

Alternative schedule: adapt to your particular timetable.

Key words

groups, local community, roles, rights, responsibilities, attitudes and values, bias, prejudice, age groups, gender groups, family, clan, kinship, marriage, rural and urban communities, local government, democracy, local level councillors, laws and rules, community services

Possible assessment tasks

The following tasks can be done on paper or as an oral report. They can be done for individual or group assessment:

1 Choose five different groups in your community. Describe each group in terms of roles, rights and responsibilities. Describe the most important values for each group.

2 Talk to friends and acquaintances. List the most common attitudes and the most important values for boys. Do the same for girls. Compare these lists. Then give examples of three roles for girls and three roles for boys that show these values and attitudes.

3 Hold debates. You may have individuals or teams debate topics. Assess students on their ability to SEE (collect information), JUDGE [UNDERSTAND] whichever side of the debate they are given, and then ACT to present their side of the debate. The key to assessment is how well students can judge points about social organisation. (Note: there are no right answers.) Give students a day or two to prepare their cases. Appraise them on their thinking and understanding when defending their side of the debate. Debrief the class after the debates.
Be sure they understand there is no single right answer, and that debates help improve knowledge whichever side you are on. Possible debate topics are:
- Small groups of two to 10 or 15 people are the most important groups in the local community **versus** Large groups of many people are the most important groups in the local community.
- Traditional roles and values are the best ones for the local community **versus** Introduced roles and values are the best ones for the local community.
- Many individuals live very well without groups **versus** Everyone needs groups to live well.

Organisation

Teacher information

Groups

A group is a set of people who have something in common and interact with each other. Students should have little trouble finding groups and finding examples of different types of groups. Primary groups tend to be small with people who feel very close to each other. Families and some clans are good examples of primary groups.

Secondary groups can be much larger and varied such as sporting associations, the Lutheran Church, the PNG Department of Education and other institutions. Formal institutions have written rules and procedures. Local councils are an example of a group that is part of the institution of government. Sometimes local councils may act in a less formal manner because they are part of a newly introduced institution. An association can be less formal. A sporting group or a political support group are both examples of associations.

Judging, understanding and analysing groups may be hard for students. A good point of entry is to explain that human beings depend on groups. Families, clans and other kinship groups are important for the early development of children. Local communities will have many examples of groups including women's, men's, sporting, religious, kinship, formal (including police, local council, aid station workers) and informal (including school friends, age-mates, casual sports and many others).

The local community

The local community is the area around the school where students, teachers and students' families work and live. Most local communities are rural and the rest are urban. Villages and stations are rural. Cities and large towns are urban locations. This means that the examples of communities will vary. The teacher can set the principles or list the points for what is a local community. The class can discuss and agree on what the boundaries for the local community should be. Again, there won't be one correct answer. The determination of boundaries may change from one year to another and from one class to another. Only the general idea will stay the same.

Students may come to see that there is no single way to define local community boundaries. Ethnic boundaries, census boundaries, economic boundaries and other boundaries are different and subject to change.

Students will find many different types of groups as they explore their community. They may find connections to larger groups. Some community groups will link to groups outside the local community. These are parts of networks. These networks provide communication and support for local groups.

Roles

Roles are based on expectations. They are based on the expectations of society and of groups in the society. A role is how a person should act in a certain set of situations or positions. It is what a person is expected to do in different social positions. By looking at themselves, students can start to understand this concept. Students have different roles every day. The role of son or daughter, the role of friend or playmate, the role of student, and the role of brother or sister are just a few examples for discussion. Having more than one role means a person has **multiple** roles. Everyone in society has multiple roles (even a hermit is also someone's son or daughter).

Role-play offers many opportunities to learn and understand. Acting in different roles is something children often do naturally. A favourite role for many children to play is hero. All roles reflect values and attitudes. They all have rights and responsibilities.

Rights

Rights are the privileges that go with a role. The role of citizen carries many rights, for example the right to vote and to publicly express an opinion. Rights may be much less formal at the local community level. They may not be clearly stated, but they are mutually understood. For example the roles of husbands and wives may have varying rights in different local communities. Students can choose any role in the community and start to explore what rights the role has.

Responsibilities

Responsibilities are the demands made on people by roles. They are the actions that the society or group expects from the role. The group can be very critical of an individual if they believe that the responsibilities have not been properly carried out. This is called social pressure. The role holder is seen to be a poor example and should not be copied by others. In some cases, a role is taken away if a person does not perform their responsibilities. In the most severe cases, the person's role can change completely, from citizen to criminal to a prisoner in jail. However, within the local community, some groups may still see this individual from a primary group perspective; for example, in the role of clan member in trouble.

Having students look at the responsibilities of a student is one of many examples that they can explore themselves. Some students may be responsible for more than studying. Student responsibilities may include helping with school clean-up, helping other students with their studies, and stopping bullying.

Attitudes

Attitudes are part of feelings and emotions as well as ideas. An attitude is the way a person feels about something. Attitudes can often change. Many students will have never closely examined their attitudes. Comparing the child and parent's attitude to work and play is a good example of a discussion topic that allows students to begin to understand how roles can shape some attitudes. Exploring what students like and dislike is another approach to exploring and examining attitudes, using the SEE – JUDGE [UNDERSTAND] – ACT process.

From evaluating family attitudes, students can progress to looking at attitudes in the community. They will be able to find many examples of common attitudes and differences in attitudes between groups. Examining attitudes in the community will help students better understand their own attitudes and areas where bias and prejudice may exist.

Values

Values carry much stronger feelings, emotions and ideas. In the extreme cases, people are willing to fight and die for values. This means that teachers must take care to build discussions based on respect for different values. Class discussions can be started by the class setting rules to ensure that values are respected. No one should be hurt because they have values that are different from others. Teachers must guard against emotional arguments.

Students will be able to identify many values in the community. They may start to see how the values help shape social organisation. Questions can help students to understand values in social organisation, such as:

- What values are held by women?
- What values are held by men?
- What are the most important values to you?
- What are the most important values to your parents?
- What are the most important values to the local police?
- What are your most important values?

Values are based on belief systems. Values do not change quickly. Many local communities in Papua New Guinea will have groups with different values. There are traditional values and many introduced values. These directly affect behaviour. People with different values will do different things.

Melanesian values can still be very strong in rural areas, especially regarding land and land ownership. These values may have changed for some urban people, who have been away from rural land for two or three generations. Other Melanesian values include giving generously. The idea that strength comes from giving may be found in both urban and rural communities, and can still be very strong. Again, as students explore the local community, they will find changing values and variation in values.

Prejudice

In looking at prejudice, the students can consider the curriculum process of SEE – JUDGE [UNDERSTAND] – ACT. Prejudice takes away the SEE part of the process, or it can use the SEE without really 'seeing'. There is no collection of facts or observation. The observations may be made on feelings, without fact or using only partial facts. In the JUDGE part of the process, prejudice is based on poor or partial analysis, or understanding something wrongly. The prejudiced person judges and acts before knowing all of the facts (or any of the facts in the worst cases). All local communities will have examples of prejudice. This often keeps groups apart and can cause many problems.

Making observations and collecting facts needs to be done carefully and accurately. Students will need to learn that there are at least two sides to every story. Prejudice comes from people thinking that they already know the answer. They JUDGE [UNDERSTAND] before they SEE. They believe that they already know that a religion, or ethnic group, or gender group, or age group, or some other group, is inferior, has bad practices or is no good. In fact, they do not really UNDERSTAND.

Bias

Bias and prejudice are very similar. Students should not worry too much about the differences at this point. Bias can be accidental or it can be done on purpose, like prejudice. For example, a student may study local community attitudes to natural hazards and only talk to three people. None of them mention flooding because they don't think it is important. Flooding may actually be a problem and the work has a bias that is accidental. The solution is to talk to more people from different parts of the local community.

Bias also includes liking or favouring something unfairly. Some attitudes and values can be biased. It is common to hear biased statements about different ethnic groups. Some are said to be lazy and others to be untrustworthy. In these examples, the attitudes could be called biased or prejudiced. Properly done, the process of SEE – JUDGE [UNDERSTAND] – ACT should minimise bias and prejudice.

Families and marriage

Local communities will have many different examples of family types. Some will be based on traditional values and some on introduced values. Many will show a mixture of values as societies are changing. Similarly examples of marriage will vary. The teacher must be very cautious not to let prejudice or bias creep in when discussing and exploring different types of families and marriages in the community. Everyone has a right to respect in the SEE – JUDGE [UNDERSTAND] – ACT process. Students will be able to research examples of different types of families and marriage with respectful understanding if they are prepared well in class.

Kinship and clans

Kinship refers to individuals who are related to each other by marriage or blood (descent). Many classrooms will have students who use different kinship systems. These can be compared and contrasted. Teachers may like to compare their own system with that of students, if these differ. Students will be able to collect material on kinship (SEE) from their families and compare (JUDGE [UNDERSTAND]) it in class. Again, there may be problems between clans. These need to be approached carefully. Students can work towards understanding why these problems occur. They may discover it is part of social organisation and work out what can be done about it. Again the teacher must be the cautious guide in this, as some of these problems have gone on for many years with violent prejudice and bias.

Groups based on gender and age

Groups based on age and/or sex are common in Papua New Guinea. Students should be able to find various examples of gender groups, age groups and gender-age groups. Many such groups are traditional, such as men's hunting groups or women's informal gatherings to make bilums. Some are combined in modern roles, such as worshippers in church services where males and females are separated in different parts of the church. Schools, religious orders, parts of the military and police all provide other good examples.

6.2.2 Economic organisation

Main ideas

Students will begin to understand ways to study wealth and how people make a living. This section provides students with a broad introduction to economic activities and how to study them. It looks at the past economic systems in Papua New Guinea and the newer systems that are being introduced. Almost everyone is interested in *bisnis*. The local community provides a good starting place to study ideas about wealth and economics. Again, economic organisation is part of social organisation; or social organisation is part of economic organisation. Different people have different ideas.

Students will be able to look for examples of the basic parts of economic organisation: land, labour, capital, technology and trade. It is important for them to understand that economic change and development has been going on for a long time. Papua New Guinea has been adapting and developing new elements of its economic systems for thousands of years.

Example of elaborating a learning outcome on social and econmic groups

Strand: Organisation

Sub-strand: Social and economic organisation

Focus: Economic organisation: the economy of Papua New Guinea today through your local community

Learning outcome: *6.2.2 Students are able to appraise the relationship between groups and the contributions they make to the local society and economy.*

- At the Grade 6 level, it is best to keep elaborations simple. There are many ways to examine how groups work socially and economically. Markets are one of the best because they directly serve both social and economic functions. They are a time to get together and a time to make money. Students can look at markets in or out of school. They can also have their own markets.
- A possible elaboration for one week:

Alternative schedule: adapt to your particular timetable.

Monday	Tuesday	Wednesday	Thursday	Friday
1 hour Organise a barter market for a school lunchtime. Have the class discuss bartering and how they could organise a barter market during a school lunch. Work out a plan and advertising campaign for a lunchtime barter market.		1 hour Implement the plan and have a barter market. Be certain students have the opportunity during the lunch market to observe and record what happens.		1 hour Discuss the results of the barter market. Did anyone cheat? Was cash used? How successful was the market?

Key words

economics, economy, cash, labour, land, technology and capital, trade, bartering, economic organisation, scarcity, extractive industries, money, consumers, formal and informal economies, subsistence, consumer, consumer society, sustainable consumption

Organisation

Organisation

Possible assessment tasks

The following tasks can be done on paper or as an oral report. They can be done for individual or group assessment:

1. Discuss or write about the contributions that each family member makes to the family. Who keeps the house clean? Who provides the food? How important are all the contributions? What would happen if some of them stopped?

2. What are the most important economic activities in the local community? Which ones make the most money? Which ones help the most people?

3. How many different types of traditional money did the community use in earlier times? Write about the history of traditional money, how people obtained and used the different types, and what has happened to them now?

4. Choose an economic activity that happens within the local community, for example, fishing, farming, running a trade store or selling newspapers. Explore how land, labour, capital and technology are used. Conclude the assignment by answering the question, 'Is this activity sustainable?'. If it is, what will it look like in the future in our community? If it is not sustainable, what will happen when it finishes?

Teacher information

Economics

Economics studies how wealth is created and how people make a living. It explores the basic areas of wealth creation: land, labour, capital and technology. There will be many examples of these in any local community for students to explore.

All local communities will have many types of **land** use, land ownership and attitudes to the value and maintenance of land. Students can explore all of these by coming to an appreciation of the basic economic forces in the community. They can begin to understand differences in attitudes and values that different groups have to land. Some land can be sold or leased. Other land is held in Melanesian systems where land belongs to a community, with many different ways to determine its use and length of use.

Comparing local examples of land ownership or use with students will help them understand how economic organisation can be different, depending on the group or society. Students can start with simple examples, for example, 'How is a government building provided with land? Who owns that land?' Students can compare this with local garden plots or homes. 'By whom and how is the land owned?' are questions that will stimulate students to think about the social and economic organisation of their local community. Again, in areas where land disputes are common, the teacher must take care to have clear discussion rules and proceed with caution on sensitive community issues.

All students are a good example of the formation of a **labour** force. Their education will eventually contribute to some parts of the local, provincial or national economy.

Other types of education or training are gained at home, in the workplace (which includes gardens and cash crop smallholdings), and in other learning situations. There are many types of work or labour, and many examples will be found in every local community.

Everyone working represents a type of labour. For example, every woman working to raise children represents one form of labour. Every person raising food in a garden represents a form of agricultural labour. Some people are paid for their labour in cash. Some are not paid with cash. It will be important for students to understand that they all contribute to the local economy in different ways.

Traditional capital might have been a small bilum filled with valuable seashells or a set of social obligations to complete an enterprise. Modern capital is the funding or money needed to start or expand a business. For example, at the local level, the person who saves or borrows to buy a PMV to start a passenger business has saved or borrowed capital. If the person has a good business, the capital can grow and another PMV is purchased or the borrowed money is repaid. If it is a bad business, the capital may be lost.

Technology has become more and more important to economies. Machines and business systems can do more and more to create capital. Often this means that people (labour) must become more and more trained to use the technology.

Four parts of an economy

One way the curriculum suggests helping students understand their economy is to divide it into four parts: primary, secondary, tertiary and quaternary sectors. This is a simplification, but helpful in the present situation where changes occur in economic systems every day and every year. There are many connections between the four parts.

Primary means first, like primary school. **Primary industry** produces raw products with little change to them. Papua New Guinea has many examples, from sea products to minerals to cash crops. Very little processing is done before they are sold.

Once primary products have been sold, processing may take place as **secondary industry**. For example, PNG gold is turned into jewellery, or copra is often used in making the base for cosmetic face creams.

In the **tertiary sector** the gold jewellery is sold. Or a wholesaler may sell a pallet or case of the face cream that has copra as its base to a retail store. The retailer in a shop or trade store then sells it to the customer. Transporting goods and selling them takes place in the tertiary sector. Tertiary refers to goods, like jewellery and face cream, and services like cleaning houses, teaching children and repairing buildings. It includes the methods by which goods and services are moved around and how they are sold.

The **quaternary sector** is new to Papua New Guinea. Students will understand it is talking about the fourth part of an economy because it comes from the word 'quarter', which is a fourth. Both words come from the same root word for four. The quaternary sector is the part of an economy that is based on information services such as computers and the World Wide Web (www). There are many urban examples of computer usage. The 'information revolution' will be harder to find in many rural areas.

Formal, informal and subsistence

People in the **formal sector** use written records and are school-trained. The **informal sector** is often made up of single sellers, artisans and traders. All of these people, however, are making a living and working at creating wealth.

The ideas of formal and informal sectors in an economy are a good way to introduce the issue of bias that can exist in economic thinking. The economists who write studies of economies tend to find it easier to identify with school-trained people like themselves. They reflect this in the terms 'formal' and 'informal'. The term 'formal' sounds positive. Informal sounds like something less. In actual fact, both are important parts of the Papua New Guinea economy. The terms show the bias of the people doing the studies and provide a good example for students to explore.

Similarly, many economists have never closely studied the informal sector. They assume that much of it is subsistence. Subsistence means to have no surplus; it means having just enough to exist. In rural communities, the class will be able to find many examples of people doing much more than subsisting. There may not be a large cash economy, but there will be many other ways of making a living, creating wealth and using it. Feasting, exchanges and the use of pigs all show how surpluses can be used in different economies.

Students can look at these traditional ways of developing and using labour, land, technology and capital. To the western-trained outsider, this may look like subsistence. That is a very biased opinion. In fact there are complex systems at work. These are now changing rapidly to become new mixed systems that use both cash and traditional ways to earn a living and produce wealth.

Money

Money is something that everyone in the community recognises as valuable and will accept for payment. There will be many examples of different types of traditional money. There will also be many examples of the different ways people use money in local communities. These include the Sunday systems of plantation workers, and other community activities of joint contributions. There are many examples of individuals saving, spending and using money to make money.

There are many ways to explore attitudes and values, prejudice and bias about money with students. One example is a common statement students may have heard —'Money is the root of all evil'. The real statement is Biblical and says that, 'The love of money is the root of all evil'. This is one of the many examples of attitudes and values that people have about money that the class can discuss. Students can discuss value issues such as, 'Is stolen money the same as money you earn from work or the same as bride price money given by a clan, family or community?'

Consumption and consumers

All local communities will have different levels and different types of consumption. That means they will consume resources differently. People in local communities will have a greater range of consumption choices when they are able to earn cash or have cash sent to them from working relatives. But all communities will have patterns of consumption for students to explore. For example, students can consider questions like: 'What are people using? What do they save for? What are they producing to consume?'

Many Papua New Guineans are only at the edge of the consumer society. Consumer societies are based on buying goods and services. People focus on having more and they want larger items. Automobiles and televisions are two examples of growing consumption. This uses up resources. The questions to ask students include, 'Is the consumer society growing in Papua New Guinea? What examples of consumerism can we see or find? How long can this behaviour be sustainable?'

Sustainable consumption has been practised for thousands of years in parts of Papua New Guinea. Students should be able to identify examples of this and search for past examples by talking to family members and others. Students should also be able to find examples of where people are rapidly using up resources or selling them for cash. They can then consider how sustainable this may be. They can explore questions such as, 'How long can some economic activities continue?' and 'What happens when these economic activities stop?'

6.2.3 Community development

Main ideas

There are many ways for students to look at development. Nations develop, people develop, and communities develop. There is no single right way or wrong way to develop. Different types of development work for different communities. People often find their own ways to develop the local economy and local social organisations. The SEE – JUDGE [UNDERSTAND] – ACT approach as part of the social science process is one way to approach development. A good outcome that can result from development is a safe and healthy environment. National, provincial and local community services can help create a safe and healthy environment.

Example of elaborating a learning outcome on community development

Strand: Organisation

Sub-strand: Social and economic organisation

Focus: Community development

Learning outcome: *6.2.3 Students are able to participate in local social and economic activities that contribute to the development of the local community.*

- Community development is a large area. It will be easy to try to do too much. Work to keep students' ideas simple. Complicated activities will have a high risk of failure.

A possible elaboration for one week:

Monday	Tuesday	Wednesday	Thursday	Friday
1 hour Each community will be different. Have a class discussion about who most needs help in the community. Think of neighbours or others who are in need. Have the class consider what could be done. Have the class choose one task that they think would be most helpful to one of the cases discussed. Have someone investigate after class to be sure the planning is appropriate.		1 hour Arrange for the class to carry out their plan, after ensuring that it is practical. The activity may take time after class to complete. (Helping provide information is one idea to consider. Remember that many people may not be able to read and that different people will need information in different languages.)		1 hour Discuss the results. How hard was it? Did the class feel it was worthwhile? Could they have done better? Are they willing to try more? (Perhaps after school?) Acknowledge problems and see what solutions the class may suggest.

Alternative schedule: adapt to your particular timetable.

Key words

community development, development recipients, scale of development, safe and healthy environment, adapting development

Possible assessment tasks

The following tasks can be done on paper or as an oral report. They can be done for individual or group assessment:

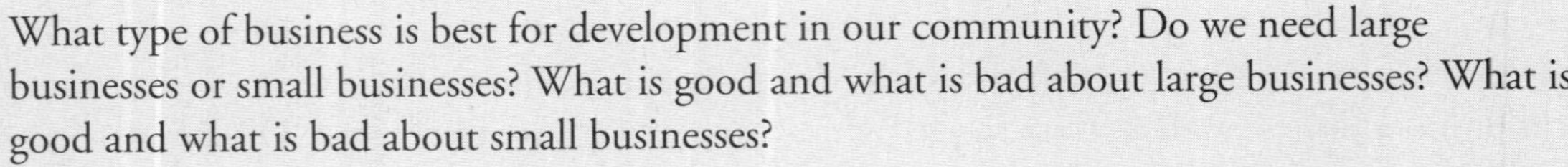

1. What type of business is best for development in our community? Do we need large businesses or small businesses? What is good and what is bad about large businesses? What is good and what is bad about small businesses?

2. Traditional land ownership is the way traditional development worked. How can traditional development be used with other types of land development in the local community?

The following tasks can be done in groups or as individuals.

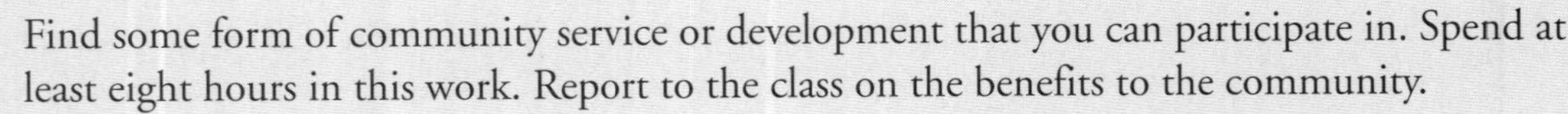

3. Find some form of community service or development that you can participate in. Spend at least eight hours in this work. Report to the class on the benefits to the community.

4. Explore your community to see what can be done to make a safe and healthy environment. Consider what is important and what you can actually do. Design a development activity to help create a safe and healthy community. Discuss it with your teacher and parents. Carry out the activity.

Teacher information

Development

Development intends to make something better. The basic idea is to make social or economic improvements to the community. For example, development may provide better health, better education or better ways to make money.

One type of development is assistance. Development can assist people to do things, live better, find work or have better health facilities. Many Papua New Guinea families practise types of assistance and this is one type of development that students can find in local communities. It is important that they understand that much development actually comes from the community.

Community development

The SEE – JUDGE [UNDERSTAND] approach allows students to look at the many local examples of development. There will be for example:

- Initiatives based on Melanesian families where families look after the sick, the aged and distant kin who need shelter or other help (Many such examples occur in the growing city populations where Melanesian family values help people become urban residents)
- Government projects, policies and community services to assist development
- Church and other NGO services
- Donor development (AusAID is a leading donor).

Students can consider if the development is good or bad. Often people will talk about positive development or positive behaviour. Basically the word 'positive' means good. People also use the word 'negative' and refer to negative behaviour or a negative outcome. What they mean is that they consider it was bad.

An example of negative development could be a village selling their tuna fishing rights for money that they quickly spend. People may consider this to be bad development because they lose the fish and soon lose the money. An example of positive or good development might be seeing glasses being made available to improve people's eyesight. There will be many other examples for students to SEE – JUDGE [UNDERSTAND] – ACT (sometimes).

Development recipients

The development recipients are the people who receive the development assistance. Again students can look at the different types of assistance. For example, it may come from a family, a clan, an NGO, a project or an enterprise. The most important thing is to have recipients closely involved in development to be sure it is appropriate.

Sometimes, when development comes from outside the community, people in the community may not actually want the development. Students may find examples of project benefits that were limited to some people only, making others unhappy. Sometimes the technologies used are not sustainable or appropriate for the recipients.

For example, health centres were given solar and gas-powered cool boxes that broke. No one knew how to repair or maintain them. The recipients were not considered. Hospitals have been given X-ray machines that needed expensive X-ray film not available in Papua New Guinea. Fishery projects for villages have built complicated ice-producing works that the local people have not been able to maintain.

Adapting development

Papua New Guinea has many examples of people doing their own development. Mutual support in families, clans and communities are examples of this. Starting up small community businesses in agriculture, tourism, retail (such as used clothing businesses) and transport are all examples of small scale economic development that people can do successfully by themselves. It is important to understand that everyone can do some things themselves. Students need to know that they and their families can make improvements themselves, rather than wait for an overseas or government project to come to them.

A safe and healthy environment

Another challenge for communities is to develop a safe and healthy environment. This requires people working together. It means the community must have the ability to organise and ensure basic needs like clean water, safe housing, good health, and education. Students can search for traditional and new ways within the community of providing a safe and healthy environment. They can SEE and JUDGE [UNDERSTAND] ways to improve these, and may find activities to ACT to have a safer and healthier environment.

Culture

About this strand

The Culture strand has one sub-strand, Cultural Expression.

Culture and cultural expression is at the heart of every community. There will be a variety of different cultures and cultural influences in every local community. Students can explore community cultural expressions, beginning with family and clan examples and moving to larger groups, using the SEE – JUDGE [UNDERSTAND] – ACT process.

Students from different cultural backgrounds can compare and contrast cultural expression. The teacher will always ensure that respect is maintained as cultural expression varies between many groups. Ethnic groups and gender groups are two areas that require particular care. Students will be able to find many examples of bias and prejudice regarding cultural expression at the local community level.

Always remind students that good social science is based on respect. Bad social science includes prejudice and bias.

Students live and breathe within the cultural environment. Sometimes this makes it difficult to see culture clearly. It is taken for granted and, until students start comparing and contrasting the different examples of cultural expression, they may have difficulty fully appreciating their own cultures. The teacher may have to guide students towards finding the richness of cultures in Papua New Guinea.

Students are also part of the changes to culture. You will need to help students see that some parts of their culture are growing very quickly. In the SEE – JUDGE [UNDERSTAND] process the class can discuss what cultures gain and lose as they change. There are no simple or right answers.

This strand closes by giving students an opportunity to participate in local community culture. Preparing for and participating in a local community event provides students with an excellent chance to review much of the social science material covered so far. Learning can be consolidated based on student actions. It completes much of the SEE – JUDGE [UNDERSTAND] – ACT process or cycle that the curriculum uses for social science.

This strand has three learning outcomes and these have been divided into three sections:

- Finding culture in our communities
- Culture changes
- Participating in local culture

An 'Example of elaborating a learning outcome' is given for each of the three sections.

6.3.1 Finding culture in our communities

Main ideas

Students can find many different examples of culture in local communities. There will also be many different cultures in some communities. All communities will have cultural expressions from different cultures. There will be physical examples of cultural expression, for example, buildings and pictures. There will be many types of social expressions, in terms of values, attitudes and organisation.

Students will explore living cultures as they appear in the local communities. They will find examples of invention or innovation, where these cultures have created new words or new art. They will also find many examples of adaptation, where features or parts of a different culture are taken and used in the local culture. Western paints may be used to colour traditional masks for example, or steel whistles used as part of a traditional singsing.

Looking for cultural expression will allow students to follow many different paths. Much will depend on their community and their focus. They can be guided towards art, music, dance, house architecture, or the cultural expressions of eating, types of food served, and comparisons between everyday eating and special ceremonial foods. Remember, all parts of a culture have value. It can be interesting to explore attitudes about what types of cultural expression are regarded as more or less valuable.

Example of elaborating a learning outcome on local culture

Strand: Culture

Sub-strand: Cultural expression

Focus: Finding culture in our communities

Learning outcome: *6.3.1 Students are able to identify and describe the basic features of local culture and cultures.*

- Elaborations can draw on the first two strands. They can explore how different cultural expressions are linked to the environment or to protecting or exploiting the environment. The economic value of cultural expressions can be explored in an elaboration. Social organisation is a part of all cultural expression.
- A possible elaboration for one week:

Culture

Monday	Tuesday	Wednesday	Thursday	Friday
1 hour Each community will be different and there may be a variety of cultures. Be sure all have a chance for expression. Discuss with the class how many cultural groups they represent. For each cultural group in the class, have that group determine what is their favourite cultural expression. If practical, have them plan to demonstrate this.		1 hour Spend this time with the cultural groups in the class allowing them to demonstrate their favourite cultural expression (for example this could be song, dance, food, dress, stories, and so forth). Some class members may be able to invite a member of their culture to the class. Discuss with the guests the type of social organisation needed to have this cultural expression. Explore any links with economic or environmental activities.		1 hour Have the class consider the different cultural expressions that have been presented. Have them consider what might be Melanesian, Western or from another culture that exists locally. How are these expressions changing? How might they adapt in the future? What will become of them in the future?

Alternative schedule: adapt to your particular timetable.

Key words

culture, living culture, innovation, appropriation, adaptation, bias and prejudice between cultures, cultural expression, special ceremonies, rites of passage, religious and spiritual practices, art, traditional art, contemporary art, sacred art, music and singing, religious music, secular music, sculpture, other carvings, painting, examples of art adapting, appropriating and innovating

Possible assessment tasks

The following tasks can be done on paper or as an oral report. They can be done for individual or group assessment:

1 How many cultures can you identify in your community? What differences do they have? How are they similar? What activities bring them together in the community?

2 Choose an adult family member or older friend and draw this person. Label the cultural influences that you can see in the drawing; now, on the reverse side of the drawing, draw this person's grandparents and label the cultural influences you can see there; finally, either on the same or a new page, write a description of what you think a person in your community will look like fifty years in the future.

3 Compare the house that you are presently living in to one from 100 years ago. What are the differences between the two? Now think how a house in your community might look in another 100 years. How different will it be? What parts of the house or things in the house will tell you about your culture?

4 Choose two radio music programs and listen to both Papua New Guinea and other music. Listen to the songs and report on what they are about. What do these songs tell you about the different cultures? Tell why you think some of the songs are more popular in your community than others. Can you find examples of attitudes, values, bias or prejudice in the songs?

5 Take the *Births, Deaths and Marriages* section of the newspaper. What different types of cultural expression can you find here? What sort of cultural expression is the newspaper itself? Explain how it is changing or adding to these ceremonies.

Teacher information

Culture

Culture is a very broad concept in social science. It includes the common ways that people think and act in a society. It includes all the physical objects that the society uses or makes. This is often called the physical culture.

There are cultures inside cultures inside cultures. Local communities will be part of larger cultures. For example, a village on the lower Sepik River is part of the Sepik culture, which can be further divided by different areas along the river into individual communities. Within the community, even the school has its own micro-culture. Students and teachers behave and are treated differently in different schools.

Papua New Guinea is a grand mix of cultures. It has influences from Western and Asian cultures, but a base of Melanesian culture. There will be examples in every local community of products, plant materials, ideas and ways of organising that can be traced back to different cultures. This offers an exciting area for students to explore and examine their own cultural background.

Living culture

Cultures are alive because the people in them are alive and continually changing. Cultures reflect the changes that groups make. Before Western influence, there were many examples of cultural change in local communities. Pottery styles changed, tattoos changed, and traditional stories tell of other changes. Students can find examples of these from older people, particularly relatives.

Change has always happened. The difference today is that it is happening very quickly with the introduction of so many cultural influences from overseas. Even so, students should be able to find examples in the past of cultures changing quickly in order to adapt. (The 'time of darkness' story is a good example from the Student Book, Chapter 3.) Today much change is occurring as a result of new technology.

Innovation

An innovation is any type of invention. It can be an idea, a new social custom, new song, dance, ornament or technology. All living cultures innovate. They make new songs or designs that may then change slowly, but they do still change. Sometimes people think that no change occurs in traditional culture. This is false. Traditional culture has been changing for thousands of years.

Students will often be able to find examples of new words in the language. These are innovations. *Tok Pisin* is a language that adds innovations all the time. In some places the new words last; in other places the new words may only be used for a few months or a year and then disappear. Many innovations do not last very long.

Appropriation

Cultural appropriation means taking or adapting something from one culture to another. There are thousands of examples of this all over Papua New Guinea, including the community six-to-six dance. The time has been appropriated from the Western clock. The style of dance and music has been appropriated from overseas and often adapted to Papua New Guinea tastes, with innovation in the form of new songs.

New types of food may be sold at the six-to-six dance. Often lamb chops or lamb fries will be cooked on a metal drum which has been cut in half. The metal drum has been changed from a storage device to a stove, so the stove is an innovation. The lamb chops have been appropriated from one culture to another. The food is then sold for kina and toea. A new system has been appropriated and placed in PNG local culture.

Appropriation is an exciting area for students to explore. They may also be able to find examples where ideas or styles have been appropriated internally between Melanesian cultures.

Adaptation

Cultures can grow and diversify through innovation and appropriation. Both forms can also involve adaptations. Adaptation takes and uses an item for a local community's particular needs. The Western money system has been adapted by using kina and toea as denominations. Just as communities adapt to the physical environment, they can adapt to other cultural practices.

Some Western church services have adapted traditional art or music to be part of the religious service.

Bias and prejudice between cultures

Communities and groups will often see their cultures as best, but there are good and bad aspects to every culture. This is a good time to further discuss bias and prejudice with students. One of the reasons that cultures change is to develop. Values and attitudes change. Students need to consider these carefully and not pre-judge cultures that are different from theirs in the local community.

Cultural expression

There will be examples of cultural expression in each local community. Local cultural expression will include body decorations, clothing, dances, songs, art, sculpture and everything else that expresses or identifies some aspect of the local culture. There will be expressions of many different types of local cultural influences.

It will be easiest for students at this level to start with Melanesian cultural expression as the base for study. But students should not be discouraged from exploring the many types of local cultural expression they may find. These will include appropriations and adaptations as well as innovations.

Special ceremonies will provide students with a way to look at the mixed cultural expressions that presently exist in local communities. Births, birthdays, ceremonies to become a man or woman, and clan ceremonies will all provide good material for discussion and comparison. Marriage is another good area for cultural expression and variation depending on the community. It can be a sensitive area and the teacher will need to carefully guide discussion. Death ceremonies in the local community will need to be approached with respect and care.

There will also be many examples in other expressions of art in the form of paintings, house decorations, body decorations, clothing, sculpture and many other areas.

Examples of art adapting, appropriating and innovating

Papua New Guineans can be very proud of their art. One of the most famous European painters of the twentieth century was Pablo Picasso. He appropriated and adapted parts of Melanesian art to his own work. This is a good example of a culture taking something from Papua New Guinea.

Many Western artists have followed Picasso and used Melanesian influences in their art. At the same time Melanesians have appropriated Western oil paints and inks and adapted them to Melanesian art. Much of the Melanesian art for tourists are adaptations for a specific market. Something that functioned originally as traditional Melanesian religious art now has a commercial function; it is a product to sell to tourists.

6.3.2 Culture changes

Main ideas

Change is rapid and happening right in front of us. For example, radio, schools, newspapers and the introduction of a cash economy are just a few influences that are changing cultures in Papua New Guinea's local communities today. This is happening in almost all parts of the world. Students will be able to find examples in areas such as dress, language, music and communication.

They can SEE and study closely what change is happening in the local community. Lively class discussion can follow as they JUDGE [UNDERSTAND] the changes. Class discussion can then look at questions like, 'How valuable are the changes? How have values changed in the local community?' Again there are many reasons and influences for change, with no single right answer about what may be good and what may be bad.

Example of elaborating a learning outcome on changing cultures

Strand: Culture

Sub-strand: Cultural expression

Focus: Culture changes

Learning outcome: *6.3.2 Students are able to identify and appraise the changes taking place in local culture.*

- Change is a major theme for the social science text. Students have looked at changes to the environment, to social and economic organisation, and now to local culture. All these strands can be tied together in discussions about changes to local culture. The task of the teacher is to make it simple enough for students to understand, but point out that there are connections to environment, society and the economy for students to consider.

A possible elaboration for one week:

Monday	Tuesday	Wednesday	Thursday	Friday
1 hour Discuss with the class what types of art can be found in the local community. For example sacred art, commercial art, traditional art and so forth. Have them plan an excursion to explore the community for art.		1 hour Take the class around the community to look for examples of art. This can include traditional art, Western art, and commercial art such as advertisements and posters. You may see pictures, see objects, hear songs and so forth. With each cultural expression of art that the class finds, discuss what changes are indicated for the culture.		1 hour Continue discussions of what the class saw and how the art can indicate changes to culture. Have students make a representation of some type of art that shows a change to culture (for example, a song, story, drawing, painting or sculpture).

Alternative schedule: adapt to your particular timetable.

Culture

Key words

reasons for change, change makers, colonial period, new religions, education, mass media, new technologies, changes to language, customs and laws, changing by example, migration, forced migration, voluntary migration, push factors, chain migration, pull factors.

Possible assessment tasks

The following tasks can be done on paper or as an oral report. They can be done for individual or group assessment:

1. Describe the colonial period in your local community. Who were the colonists and what changes to local culture did they make?
2. Hunt for new words and phrases. See if they can be found in the media. Look for ones specific to your local community. Check with older people for new words and phrases that they remember coming into the language. Think about the changes that these new words and phrases signify. What changes do the new words indicate about the community? Give as full an explanation as you can for each new word or phrase.
3. Give the reasons why people are migrating to or from the local community. What changes does this make to local cultures?
4. Describe the changes to local culture that have occurred since you started school to now. Then write about the earlier changes to local culture, from when your parents started school.

Teacher information

Reasons for change or change makers

People and local communities have always been changing. Students should recognise that one reason for change is the education they are receiving. The difference with change today is the speed at which it is happening. New technologies for transportation and communication are speeding the pace of change.

The reasons for change or change makers can also be called agents of change. Some important ones include colonisation, missionaries, education, mass media, new technologies, migration and population growth. Students can look at each item separately, but will need to understand and explore how they are combined. For example, population growth is a consequence of a combination of items. These include better health technologies, new education curriculum, mass media programs, economic developments and other changes. Each item can be analysed in this way.

The colonial period

Every local community will have some examples that students can find of changes introduced by colonisation. (The amount of examples located may depend on the SEE and JUDGE [UNDERSTAND] activities that students have time for.) Colonisation may have been Australian, German, British or Japanese. There may be also be different combinations, depending on the place.

New religions

Examples of religions bringing change to the community will be very common. Missionaries have brought churches and various services including health, education and recreation. Some new religions have introduced businesses. Students will be able to find many new influences from new religions. They may also find innovation and appropriation where traditional practices appropriate parts of the new religions, or the new religions appropriate and adapt parts of the traditional culture to their religious and other services.

Education

You can use your own school to show how education makes changes to the local community. Using your own classroom is a good example to promote discussion with students. Compare what may have been happening 50 years ago and 150 years ago. Let students use their imaginations to describe what might have been happening on the same piece of ground where their school now stands. To see how much change has taken place, let them imagine what the people who stood on the school grounds 50 and 100 years ago could look forward to. Then look at what the students' own future might hold. This is a good way to show how fast changes are occurring.

The mass media

Use any examples of mass media that may be available locally. Radio and newspapers are probably the most common items. There may be limited numbers of books. Explore the content with students to see what is changing now. Have students SEE – JUDGE [UNDERSTAND] the values and attitudes that can be found in the locally available mass media.

Films, books, video, television, the World Wide Web and DVDs are other examples of mass media that are available in some local communities for students to explore and discuss. It is particularly important to alert students to the many different values and attitudes that the mass media brings to the local community. Discuss how this can influence change.

Changes to language

New words and expressions are invented every day. Some of these innovations may only last a year and be limited to a local community. Sometimes they will only have meaning to a family or clan. Other words and phrases become part of the mainstream language. Most Papua New Guineans speak at least two languages. The class should be able to find many examples of changes to language, language usage and phrases. Even schoolyard slang is an example of innovation or adaptation.

Customs and laws

Western laws introduced during the colonial period have forced Papua New Guineans to change. Sometimes the laws were adapted to local custom. Both customs and laws have changed since Independence. Again the amount of change will vary in each local community. Students should have no problem finding examples of laws that have changed people and customs.

Changing by example

The idea of changing by example should be easy to explore in the local community. There are always trendsetters. The trend of people wearing hats is an example. One day no one will have a hat. The next day someone sets an example by wearing a hat and many others quickly follow. Students should be able to hunt out examples (SEE) and discuss the reasons for them (JUDGE [UNDERSTAND]). Copying what they see other people do is a very important way that people change culture.

Migration

Almost every school will have an example of a migrant. This is an agent of change. Migrants bring new ways of thinking, different cultural expressions and often have a different language. This enriches and allows for cultural change.

All communities will have some history of migration. People will have arrived and people will have moved on. A study of the history of local communities should also find examples of past migration. Again, migration and change have been taking place since humans first started local communities in Papua New Guinea. Challenge students to find out as much as they can about the history of the local community. Every community will have an interesting history of migration. Remember that early migrants left Papua New Guinea islands to settle many areas in the Pacific Ocean. These were brave people. Many perished but others succeeded to travel through the New Guinea islands and beyond.

6.3.3 Participating in local culture

Main ideas

This section allows students a chance to participate in their local culture or cultures. They will have further opportunities to SEE, JUDGE [UNDERSTAND] and then ACT in some cultural activity. It can be a traditional cultural event, a transitional event or students may participate in contemporary cultural events. The key point is that all aspects of this culture belong to them, as it does to their local community. There may be a wide variation in events depending on the different cultural backgrounds in the class. This is a good area for discussion. It may reflect the local community's cultural mix.

Example of elaborating a learning outcome on cultural participation

Strand: Culture

Sub-strand: Cultural expression

Focus: Participating in local culture

Learning outcome: *6.3.3 Students are able to participate in local culture.*

- Participating in a local cultural event allows students to be part of the community. It also provides a good chance to review much of the material on social organisation. Students can begin to see the connections between culture and their studies in earlier strands. The suggested elaboration can be limited to two hours of class time, with an optional third hour for class discussion.
- The time for observing and participating in cultural events will have to be additional or extra time out of school volunteered by students. There may be opportunities to invite different cultural groups to observe each other's events. This will add to the richness of class discussions. Teachers may expand class time for additional discussion on how the cultural event or events apply to previous study material.

Monday	Tuesday	Wednesday	Thursday	Friday
1 hour Hold a class discussion on the different cultures represented in the class and the different cultural events that occur in the local community. Either as a single group or as a set of groups, decide on which events will be good for class participation and possible viewing. Have the group or groups determine what will be necessary for participation and make a participation plan. (Actual participation and/or observation will have to be done out of class time.)		1 hour After participating and observing cultural events, have the class discuss them in terms of roles taken by the people in the event. Have them discuss the purpose of the event. Is it purely social? Is there an economic side to it? Does it help people to live together better or feel better or understand better? Have the students see how many different kinds of cultural expression they can identify as part of the event (for example, special clothing, special language, stories, art, decoration, songs, music and other cultural expressions). Have them consider the values and attitudes that the event expresses.		1 hour Optional further discussions on how the cultural events link to other parts of social science studies. For example, is there an environmental component? Does the event adapt to the environment? Is there a strong economic component? Is the event helping us to better understand relationships between men and women? If so, what does it tell us about them?

Alternative schedule: adapt to your particular timetable.

Key words

cultural event, oral, stories, song, music, dance, drama

Possible assessment tasks

The following tasks can be done on paper or as an oral report. They can be done for individual or group assessment:

1 Report on participating in a local cultural event. Include the type of preparation needed and the skills that people needed to play different roles in the event. What were the results of participation?

2 Collect stories and/or songs about traditional events to perform for the class and explain why they are important to the culture.

3 Have the class find traditional stories and develop them into plays. Depending on the size of the class and the cultures of the students, students can work in one group or different smaller groups. When their drama is ready, students can present it to other classes.

Teacher information

Student safety and participation

Student safety is an important item for consideration. Take care that students can participate safely in local cultural events. Once safety concerns are addressed, there are many events for students to research, from simple story telling at the family or clan level, to larger and more organised occasions. For example, Independence or provincial celebrations may provide the class with an opportunity to sing, dance, tell a story or act out a drama.

There are many other cultural events that occur in local communities such as birthdays, feasts, dances, plays, movies, drama, sporting events, political rallies and others. Students may be welcome at some of them and may be able to volunteer some services. Let the students explore (SEE) and offer ideas for participation (JUDGE [UNDERSTAND]). Then they can ACT and discussion can follow on what the action achieved.

STRAND 4 Integrating Projects

About this strand

The Integrating Projects strand has one sub-strand, Societies and Communities. This strand provides students with an opportunity to apply a selection of everything they have learned to a project. There is the opportunity to do this within the local community and/or to explore links between the community and the province.

Links between the province and local communities will be strong or weak depending on many factors. Some communities are geographically isolated from the provincial centre and others may have weak links for other reasons.

Teachers should work to keep projects simple and effective. Effective means that there is an actual visible or measurable result from the project. This will allow the projects to serve two very important purposes:

- Students will use the knowledge and skills learned from social science in a practical application.
- Students will get a sense of satisfaction from their results as they see their efforts directed at a real concern rather than just a school exercise.

  A teacher will know that an integrated project is successful if these two measures are met: students using their knowledge and achieving some real-life result.

  This strand has two learning outcomes and these have been divided into two sections:

- Different ways to study your community
- Connections between the province and its communities

An 'Example of elaborating a learning outcome' is given for each of the two sections.

6.4.1 Community student project work

Main ideas

There are many ways to study a community. Each community will have many different areas where students can work to improve community life. They may choose to look at people and the environment, or social-economic organisation or some other part of culture. It is important to stimulate and encourage students to follow their interests. This may mean dividing students into several groups, especially if the integrating projects are culturally oriented. Again, this can be a time for class sharing.

Example of elaborating a learning outcome on community improvement

Strand: Integrating Projects

Sub-strand: Societies and communities

Focus: Different ways to study your community

Learning outcome: *6.4.1 Students are able to improve the life of the community by gathering and evaluating information about it and taking appropriate action.*

- Students may be able to improve community knowledge, assist with community clean-ups, record other local cultural expressions, help improve local market facilities, and complete other types of assistance to the community.
- The curriculum allocates three hours a week to Social Science. This means that some portion of the project time will have to be done after class. It may also be possible to combine the project with another curriculum subject.

Monday	Tuesday	Wednesday	Thursday	Friday
1 hour Discuss with students whether they will work as one group or several groups to do a study project on preserving traditional stories from different cultures found in the class. Listen carefully to the class ideas and have them agree on one or several collection groups. Go over the SEE–JUDGE [UNDERSTAND] –ACT process and expand it to the social science process. Give students time to carry out the study (SEE).		1 hour Discuss the study results (JUDGE [UNDERSTAND]) and the possible actions that can be done to maintain the stories as part of the cultural expression of the community. For example, help preserve community culture by having the stories or histories typed and sent to a library with the best class illustrations accompanying them.		1 hour ACT to preserve the cultural material in a sustainable way. Evaluate the importance of the material in teaching the community and future generations about their cultural history.

Alternative schedule: adapt to your particular timetable.

Key words

local community project, social science process, observation, gathering information, evaluation, trying solutions

Possible assessment tasks

The task for this section is to complete an integrating project. Assessment should be ongoing during the entire project. A teacher may decide on criteria for different stages of the project. These will vary depending on the type of project a group or class undertakes. Project choice may also depend on what other classes are doing. It will be important to coordinate between subjects to ensure that students have enough time to complete all activities. Some teachers may agree on combined projects where there is a large overlap. It will then be important to separate the social science content for evaluation (from *Making a Living* for example).

It may be possible to start an integrating project while studying another strand. This will depend on the level of class abilities, time available and teacher initiative. For Grade 6, it will not be common.

Assessment could be based on three steps:

1 The first step, SEE, would evaluate how well the student has gathered information.

2 The second step would evaluate how well the student has analysed the information and come to a conclusion. How well does the student JUDGE [UNDERSTAND]? Is the conclusion logical?

3 Finally, step three, ACT, would evaluate the action. Note that science can fail; so too social science can fail. In other words, the action may not work. The assessment should not affect the student's marks if the student learns from the action and answers why it did not work. This way the student will learn that science and social science both learn by success and failure. The learning is what the student should be assessed on.

Teacher information

Social science process

The curriculum has followed the SEE – JUDGE [UNDERSTAND] – ACT process. This can now be expanded to cover an integrating project. It can be built from observations that students make on their local community. Depending on what is happening in other classes, the teacher may wish to focus on one strand in particular or give students a completely free choice.

Here is one example of following the social science process.

1. Identify the problem or need in the community.
   Example:
   - A student (or the class) observes that the local community market is very muddy and wet every time it rains and hears community members complaining about this.
2. Decide on questions.
   Example:
   - Is the wet and muddy market a problem for people?
   - Do sellers lose money because many buyers go away when it rains?
   - Why does the market get so muddy?
   - What do people think could be done?

3. Select ways of gathering information.
   Example:
   - Asking the buyers and the sellers with a short questionnaire
   - Observing what happens when it rains
   - Talking to the community officials and others who might help with solutions.
4. Divide up the class and decide on tasks for collecting information.
   Example:
   - Being sure all types of buyers (male and female) are questioned
   - Carefully observing what happens when it rains
   - Being sure all knowledgeable officials are spoken to (those in charge of the market, those with community funds, NGOs and others).
5. Analyse and evaluate the information.
   Example:
   - Have the class report on what they have found. How serious is the problem?
   - Was it really a problem or are people not so concerned about it?
6. Suggest solutions.
   Example:
   - What are the possible solutions and how much will they cost? Can the community afford the solutions or sustain them?
   - Who is available to help with the solutions? Do we need outside assistance?
   - If only a small part of the problem can be solved at once, is it worth doing a little and hoping people will continue to do a little until the whole problem is solved?
7. See if the solutions work.
   Example:
   - Students work by themselves or with others to have the problem fixed, depending on the chosen solutions. This might be seeking funding for better drainage or roofing, helping with better design and use of space, or other solutions.
   - During the process, students should keep careful notes to write up the process.

6.4.2 Connections between the province and its communities

Main ideas

The *Social Science Grade 6* focus has been on the local community. The study now expands. This final section provides a linkage to *Social Science Grade 7* that focuses on the province. It can be seen as a way to briefly introduce the larger provincial region to students.

There are many possible connections between local communities and the province. Students can explore how their local community contributes to the 'life of the province'. Teachers may wish to start with the class by discussing what makes up the life of the province. Ask: 'What makes a province? What is in it that keeps it going or keeps it alive?' From there, discussion about the links and contributions made by the students' local community can follow.

Example of elaborating a learning outcome on provincial and community connections

Strand: Integrating Projects

Sub-strand: Societies and communities

Focus: Connections between the province and its communities

Learning outcome: *6.4.2 Students are able to identify and describe how local communities contribute to the life of their province.*

- Time may be short for this final linking section. It links the community to the province, and provides an overview for the students who will continue from Grade 6 to Grade 7. The elaboration is limited to an hour.

Monday
1 hour Invite a provincial official to speak to the class and explain links between the local community and the province. Have the official cover what services the province provides for the community and how these are paid for. Have the class ask questions (some of these can be prepared beforehand as homework).

Alternative schedule: adapt to your particular timetable; ask more than one official to visit the school.

Key words

government, population, economy, culture, social organisation

Possible assessment tasks

The following tasks can be done on paper or as an oral report. They can be done for individual or group assessment:

1. Why is it important to vote in the provincial elections? Explain who you think would be the best candidate for the local community.
2. How important are provincial governments? Some people have suggested that Papua New Guinea abolish provincial governments. What would happen without provincial governments?
3. What contributions does the provincial government make to your community?

Teacher information

Types of links and contributions

Different communities will contribute in different ways to the life of the province. For each local community, students can explore links to various provincial services, including education, health, law and order, business, and resource and agricultural development. All communities will have links to the province through government, population, economic, cultural and social organisation.

The National Capital District will have special circumstances for students to explore; other schools will normally be linked to the provincial education department for part of their educational services. There will be similar arrangements with some other provincial departments.

Government links

The clearest link to provincial government is that all registered adults have the right to vote in their provincial elections. The provincial legislature makes laws that the people in the provinces must obey.

Population as a contributor

In terms of population, everyone should be counted as a provincial resident in the national census. This helps determine how service resources are allocated. The size of populations may also indicate one part of the tax base for provincial taxes. This leads to economic participation.

Economic links and contributions

Everyone is a part of the economy in one form or another. Each local community is producing something and assisting in the circulation of cash in the provincial economy. These are open economies and community contributions will vary.

Social organisation and culture

Everyone shares in the cultures and social organisations that make up the province. Students should find many links between the province and their local community in terms of shared cultures and social connections. These can be a major part of the life of the province.

Glossary

anthropology study and comparison of societies, particularly isolated and remote societies in the past. The people who practice anthropology are called anthropologists. Ask students if they have seen one in a Papua New Guinea village. Many anthropologists come to Papua New Guinea because there are so many different cultures and ethnic groups here.

catastrophic a major disaster, something very bad and damaging.

demography study of populations. A demographer is the name for a person in this type of social science. Demographers study population growth, birth rates, death rates and many other aspects of population. Demographers are often in charge of doing the census. Papua New Guinea now has over five million people with a rapidly growing population. Demographers study this type of growth and the impact it may have. For example, a demographer may study how quickly student numbers are growing to see how many new schools or teachers may be needed.

economics study of wealth and how people make a living. Economists study how wealth is produced and distributed. Papua New Guinea has many types of economic systems. Cash is now becoming increasingly important everywhere. Cash is a type of money that uses paper bills and coins. People used seashells, salt and pigs for money in the past. The subject Making a Living covers aspects of economics.

elaborate to elaborate is a verb. It means to add information. A person who hears a story might ask the storyteller, 'Can you elaborate on the ending?' The person is asking if the storyteller can give more information. The curriculum uses the term 'elaboration' in this sense, meaning to give more information. The word elaborate can also be an adjective, meaning complex or complicated. This is not the usage in the curriculum.

elaboration to give more information on a topic; to study further

fallow agricultural land that is given a rest. It is not cropped so that soils and future yields will improve.

gender refers to the sex of an individual, female or male.

gender studies looks at males and females in society. Men and women have different opportunities. Some groups are restricted to male or female participation. For example, you might discuss with students if they have noticed how women often do one type of activity and men are responsible for another. Then ask if the same occurs for boys and girls.

geography studies the locations of both land and people. Geographers ask where is it, and why? Geographers study the patterns made on the land by groups of people. They study the changes that people make to the land. They can also look at the effects that the land has on people. Much of Strand 1 is about geography. It should open discussion for students about their land or environment. See if they can think of how it might change them (For example, you can discuss clothes, food, games or work that might be different because of where a person lives.)

hermit a solitary person who lives alone with little or no interaction with other people; a person who avoids all social contact and society.

history study of the past. Historians often use social science as part of their research. The historian generally uses written records. Prehistorians study the distant past when no written records existed. History and prehistory can help us understand what happened in the past. Discuss with students the idea that people should not repeat mistakes if they know what mistakes were made by people in the past. Discuss other ways that history can help people.

political science study of government, politics and power. Political scientists study leaders, political parties and political systems. They are interested in how people vote. At age 18 students will be able to vote as citizens of Papua New Guinea. A wise voter knows about government. You can discuss with students how much they will know about government. Political science can help.

sociology study of societies and how they work. It looks at the beliefs and values that people have in a society. Sociologists often look at social problems like crime, or drinking alcohol and driving. They study what this does to people and their communities. One of the first sociological studies was about suicide. The study found that there was more suicide in some groups of people than in others. You can discuss with students why that might be the case.

There are many other special studies in social science. All study different parts or features of groups. Remind students that the group or community can be looked at in many different ways and it is important to do this. If students look at only one part of it, they won't see the community clearly. It is important to consider the many branches of social science when we look at the groups and activities all around us.

Appendices

Appendix 1: Lesson planning table

Outcomes	Things to work from and plan for
1. Learning outcome	Identify the outcome in the curriculum that you are working from.
2. Content: topic or key concept	Base this on the outcome. Decide on a theme, from other curriculum areas if appropriate, for example, our local culture.
3. What will learners learn in the particular lessons?	How will learners achieve the learning outcome? • what knowledge will they learn? • what skills will they learn? • what values and attitudes will they adopt?
4. Number of lessons that need to be taught	How many lessons do you plan to teach on this particular topic?

Assessing progress	Things to think through
1. Evidence of learning	What you will look for in each learner's work? Write down the assessment objectives. (Each one should be something a learner can do.)
2. The way learning will be assessed	Examples of what procedures you may use: • formal (oral or written presentation) • informal (teacher observation) • small task within a larger project • homework • test

Classroom practice	Things to consider
1. Method or activity	What will you do and what will learners do, and in what sequence?
2. Time	For how long will you explain or model new concepts? For how long will learners do each activity?
3. Teaching methods	How exactly will you arrange learners? • as a whole group? • working in pairs? • working individually?
4. Resources needed	Where will learners be? • in the classroom? • outside? **List any resources you may need for students to complete tasks.**

Appendix 2: Yearly plan

Units of work	Term 1	Term 2	Term 3	Term 4
Speaking and listening	Outcome… Indicator…			
Reading				
Writing				

Appendix 3: Term plan

Week	Outcomes	Student tasks	Required resources	Assessment procedures
1–3				
4–6				
7–10				

Appendix 4: Lesson plan

Teaching group √	Required Materials
Individual Whole class Team group	
Learning Strategies	**Specific Content—lesson plan Collaborating**
Interpreting Predicting Planning √ Investigating Recording √ Justifying Changing Communicating √	
Curriculum Strand	**Assessment strategy**
Cross-Curricula Strands	**Cross-Curricula activities**

Appendix 5: Assessment strategies

Sample 1: Cognitive skills template

LEARNING SKILLS ASSESSMENT CHECKLIST

For assessing learning skills, group communication skills and attitudes

NAME: **DATE:**

Skills	Skills observed √	Comments
Learning skills • can form and ask questions • can follow instructions • can find information • can find required information • can express ideas clearly and correctly • can critically reflect on own work • can organise oneself efficiently • understands how to improve own work • manages use of time well		
Group Skills • follows group rules • works cooperatively within a team • contributes to discussions without dominating • listens while other people speak • accommodates different points of view		
Attitudes • respects other students' points of view • participates freely in activities • works in a constructive and positive way • values the beliefs held by other students